The Life In Common: And Twenty Other Sermons

Edward Everett Hale

Anal.

THE LIFE IN COMMON

AND

TWENTY OTHER SERMONS

Preached in the

SOUTH CONGREGATIONAL CHURCH,

BOSTON,

BY EDWARD E. HALE.

BOSTON.

ROBERTS BROTHERS, 299 WASHINGTON STREET.

1880.

These sermons, as a careful reader would see at once, were preached Sunday by Sunday, in the regular course of religious service, and have not been selected from any long period. They were printed, week by week, as soon as they were delivered. To meet the convenience of those who wish to preserve them, a few copies are now published together.

The First Series, published in the same way, was called From THANKSGIVING to FAST. It consisted of the sermons preached in the Winter of 1878 — 1879. This series, including one or two of the sermons of 1878, covers the remainder of the year 1879. The sermons of 1880, until the summer, are collected in a similar series, under the title, THE KINGDOM OF GOD and other sermons.

The sermons preached on the Communion Sundays have been reserved for another collection.

E. E. H.

CONTENTS.

_⌐/·⌐_

THE LIFE IN COMMON.

A SERMON

PREACHED BEFORE THE UNITARIAN CONFERENCE AT
WEIR'S LANDING, N. H.

BY

Rev. E. E. HALE,

MINISTER OF THE SOUTH CONGREGATIONAL CHURCH, BOSTON.

BOSTON:
GEO. H. ELLIS, PRINTER, 101 MILK STREET.
1879.

THE LIFE IN COMMON.

No man liveth to himself, and no man dieth to himself. — ROM. XIV., 7.

The solidarity of the human race is one of the essential central truths which is revealed anew to men in all occasions of crisis. When men are enjoying a short prosperity, when they are making ready for swift calamity, in their recklessness they forget this central law, and drift back into individualism, selfishness, and similar self-culture, or other forms of deviltry.

The word "solidarity" is a new one, invented by the French authors of our time. The truth expressed is as old as Christianity.

"No man liveth to himself, and no man dieth to himself."

."All ye are brethren."

"He has made of one blood all nations of men."

"Bear ye one another's burdens, and so fulfil the whole law of Christ."

"No man said that what he had was his own, but they regarded all property as given to them in trust for the public weal."

Such are statements of this truth in the language of the New Testament.

The truth is, that this certainty of a common life was one of the three great novelties which the Christian apostles carried into the popular life of the Roman Empire, and by which they took possession of Europe and made it over. In Dr. Newman's celebrated book on the "Development of Doctrine," he admits that that theory is philosophical which says there was an original Christian gospel which has been clouded and disguised by the corruptions of later centuries. But he dismisses it with a sneer, till some one will state what this original Christian truth is. The Liberal Church accepts that challenge. It says that that original Christian truth is the immanent presence of God,— God living in man, and man living in him,— it is the certainty of infinite or immortal life, and it is this common life of brethren, the life in common, in

which all men are one. In Gibbon's celebrated account of
the rapid diffusion of Christianity, the popularity of the notion
of immortal life is dwelt upon as the chief reason for the success of the new sect, which made it cease to be a sect. But
it was immediately replied by his critics, that this was not a
novelty; that if the apostles could not have made men sure
of this, it would have been as idle a gospel as the sixth book
of the Æneid, which rests on the same hypothesis. The two
other distinctions, which Gibbon scarcely alludes to, were
what, in our Unitarian phrase, we call The Fatherhood of
God and The Brotherhood of Man. Here were three statements of life, which were made in the preaching of those
days in such direct and simple fashion that people understood them when they were made and were sure of
them. And these statements were to the world of that
time wholly new.

I. That man lived in God, moved in God, and in God had
his being,—
That God moved in man, lived in man, and gave to man
his being,—
This certainty of the God-man, or the God in man, was
revelation indeed to those poor pagans of Greece and Rome,
as it is revelation to this hour. To that great certainty
belongs the other certainty with which we have now to do.
It belongs to it, but is not the same. This truth,—that
man with man must live, that no man can live alone or die
alone, that love, sympathy, tenderness, charity, are not
merely luxuries or ornaments of life, but are the very
centre of life,—this certainty changed the world from an
obedient empire to be a well-knit commonwealth. It was
in this certainty that there impended the overthrow of every
institution then existing, and in the mere proclamation of
which all things became new.

II. It is no business of mine to go into history, and show
that the world owes to Jesus Christ this notion of the life in
common,—though this is true. My business to-day is rather,
in familiar illustrations from to-day's life, to show how often
our failures result from our forgetting this doctrine of the life
in common ; to show, again, that we succeed, as we ought to
succeed, when from the wanderings of our thought we return
to this truth. I expect to show that our failures of to-day in
ʼʼractice are largely due to a central failure here.

If to our pleasant summer meeting here we had invited a teacher of natural history to speak to us about these creatures around us; if he told us of one of these ants who are burrowing there in the path before me, that it was impossible for that ant to live away from the nest of his brethren, we should believe him. If any one tried the experiment of singling out an ant, of putting him in a gallery by himself, though with the most apt supplies of sugar and grain and water and sand and gravel, the ant would die. And we should all say, "Of course the ant would die; because, of course, ants must live in common life. The ant is a gregarious animal." And if our teacher, at any time, should point out to us a flock of wild geese passing over our heads, and should tell us that they were all bound together by a certain tie, even mysterious, that all must pass to the North together or pass to the South together, and that no separate goose could be taught or trained to endure a separate isolation, we should believe that that was a determined, unchangeable fact of nature. "Oh, yes," we should say; "of course, the wild goose also is a gregarious animal." And so if he said the same of one of these bees, trying for his honey in the flowers here, we should say, "Of course, of course; there never was a bee who lived alone, or could live alone. Bees must live together, because, of course, you know, bees are gregarious animals." It is only when Jesus Christ and his apostles assert the same thing of the race of men, that men try to escape from the law. "These are poetical expressions," they say. "This is oriental language. This is metaphorical or imaginative." But, all the same, they tell the eternal truth. The actual experiment, whether it sentence Alexander Selkirk to an island, or some wretched convict to solitary life in a prison cell, comes out always in the same way. Manhood, real life, ceases, in every effort to separate man from man. Every effort to escape the universal law fails, whether it is made by a tyrant, on the one hand, in the solitude of his palace, a hermit in the solitude of his retirement, or a miser in the solitude of his submission. True, such efforts will be repeated, till the establishment of what we call God's kingdom. But, with every effort, the experiment will fail.

I could not ask for more simple illustrations of "The Life in Common," as some of the noble witnesses of the Middle Ages called it, than I have around me here in the simple annals of the Christian democracies which planted half the early towns of New England. A dozen or two men and women, tired of the crowd, it may be of the inequality of their old life, would take up perhaps a township here in the hills, perhaps a section of a township, and go out together into the wilderness. Who is leader? There is no leader. They bear each other's burdens. Together they lift the logs for each other's houses. Together they make the frame for the school-house. Together they bridge the streams. Together they cut out the roads. When the return of the spring comes round, they meet, and they assign to each other a certain direction in such cares; but it is on the understanding that each owes something to all. There must be five selectmen, there must be three school-committee men, there must be a surveyor of highways in each district, there must be a keeper of the pound, and so on; but this is not because these are to be so many masters, but so many servants, in the little State. I could name here such a town not far away, where, when I knew it, the eight voters distributed thus among themselves the fifteen town offices. You know the success which followed such beginnings. In such beginnings might be read the history of half the towns in New Hampshire. Contrast that with the failure of some capitalist who by accident or adventure.finds himself the owner of thirty thousand acres of wild land. He selects some one who says he is used to the wilderness, and bids him enlist and lead a colony. And this man hires adventurers who will go — for pay. Will they survey a road? Yes, if he will pay them. Will they bridge a swamp? Yes, if he will pay them. Will they raise the school-house? Yes, if he will pay them. You know what the end is. When the master's money is gone, these fair-weather settlers are gone; and at the end of the generation the surveyor himself cannot find the roadways of the deserted colony. Such a contrast, in the affairs of our own local history here, is repeating itself all through history, in the difference between the success of men who work together and the failure of those who try to work alone.

In the life of cities, the same success has recently asserted itself in the establishment in England of the co-operative stores in retail trade. People complain of high prices and of wasted stocks. And then some shrewd observers, feeling their way with care, ask, " Have you ever tried a little Christianity? "* There is not a great deal of Christianity, but there

*" We cannot keep this house warm," said Mr. Skrimpington. " Have you ever coals?" said the Bachelor. — *Bachelor of the Albany.*

is some, and enough to give to the experiment its success. In a co-operative store, each man bears a part of the others' burdens, and has a part of his burden borne by the others. What results? Why,— in the language of the world,— all expense for advertising is unnecessary, all adulteration of goods becomes absurd, all expense for obtaining showy warehouses is done away with, nothing is lost by bad trade, and the business is as steady as the rise and flow of the tides,— its amount as easily predicted and provided for. When such advantages are secured, even any child of earth and time admits, has to admit, that they are worth securing. Then the idealist, the child of the spirit, tells him that such are just the sort of advantages which Jesus Christ promised to men if they would once live in the life in common. He promised life more easy and life more large, and he meant every-day life as much as life in the interstellar spaces. Of which promise of his, one visible illustration — not a very large one, but very distinct just now — is the steady abandonment through England, for this system of co-operation, of that old, cut-throat, stand-and-deliver theory of retail trade in which each dealer was hoping for his neighbor's failure,— a system resting on Adam Smith's famous gospel of selfishness, in which every man cares for himself, and no man is his brother's keeper. The success of the co-operative system of shop-keeping proves to come just in proportion to the amount of its Christianity. It succeeds, that is, just in proportion as it invites poor with rich, weak with strong, the small purchaser with the large purchaser, to share in its benefits. The failure of the efforts to carry what is called "co-operation" into manufacture has followed just in proportion to their neglect of this catholic welcome of all. Such efforts have been confessedly based on the union of workmen alone, and they have intentionally left out-of-doors the capitalist, who is, after all, a part of the body, and an essential part. Were it only in Menenius Agrippa's homely analogy of the belly in the midst of the members, the analogy which St. Paul himself adopts, we must not try to do without the organ that unites the others. Nor can we dispense with those convenient forces between, the enterprisers, the undertakers, the middle-men,— much abused, but all the same inevitable,— who bring together the sluggish forces of drowsy and timid capital, and the shifty resources of quick and passionate industry. I venture the prophecy that co-operation will succeed in manufacture, when capitalist, middle-man, and laborer find a Christian plan of bearing each other's burdens. Till then, all half-way plans fail, and ought to fail; for they are not really plans of co-operation. You need in your company Zacchæus and Matthew as much as you need the leper and the fisherman. You need the wife of Herod's secretary of the treasury as much as you need Mary Magdalen.

III. These are illustrations which are handy for our use because they come from affairs here which are passing right under our own eyes, though they are not so important as illustrations which I might have taken from the wider walks of history. At all periods of crisis, as I said, men have to come out again on the great central principle. But when we are not in crises, when things are going on in the dog-trot way, there is enough selfishness among men to make them try to avoid the eternal laws; and danger comes in in the same proportion. It is the special business of the Liberal Church, because it has always in its charge the maintenance of the simplicity of religion, to guard against these dangers. And I shall speak now of those two which press upon us most heavily because in the very nature of things they result from the tenets of the two strongest ecclesiastical bodies, except our own, which work in this community. The danger of individuality or selfishness presses us, on the one side, in proportion as the Orthodox theology is consistently maintained, and, on quite another side, it presses upon us in proportion as the Roman Catholic Church gains power in our affairs.

1. The consistent preaching of the Orthodox theology runs always into an appeal to the selfishness of the hearer. By whatever urgency, by whatever hope of heaven, by whatever fear of hell, he is asked, first and last, to save his own soul, or to inquire if it be not in danger. So entirely does the necessity for this appeal pervade all the organizations based on this theology that when especial effort is made to renew or quicken the work of an Orthodox church, that effort is made by personal appeals to individuals to save their own souls. I would be willing to ask any distinguished revivalist if he do not consider his duty, on such an occasion, to be personal. He would tell me that he fixed his eye on some one or other individual in his congregation, hoping to quicken him personally to a duty to himself. The saving of his soul is the first and is the last; it is the one object of consideration and appeal. A very desirable object, certainly. But so presented, the whole spirit of selfishness is roused just when it

ought to be suppressed. I have here the covenant by which members are now admitted into a prominent and historical orthodox church. I do not name it, because to single it out from a thousand would be invidious. It is one of those covenants made under Whitfield's influence. The earlier covenants of the Puritan fathers were broad as heaven itself. But in this modern covenant, there is not a syllable about any obligation or any life outside the handful of people who make that church. You would not know that there was any world outside of them. You would not guess that there was any great kingdom of God. They live for themselves. I do not wonder when I see such a church as that die for itself. For in any such system, as the inevitable result of the theology on which it is founded, the life in common, this central power of the Christian system, dies out and is forgotten. Now take the analogy I used before, and test this system. Suppose a teacher of the ant bade him care for himself, think of himself, and live for himself. Suppose a teacher of the migrating bird or of the hard-working bee gave such counsels. Suppose such counsels were obeyed to the letter, what becomes either of bee or of swarm,— either of bird or of flock,— either of ant or of ant-hill ?

On an occasion like this which collects us together, we must remember and resolve that the Liberal Church is always to reassert the Christian position. It is organized for the life in common. It lives and works for the life in common. The little child in the Sunday-school is to be told to be good. Yes,— but to be good why ? Because he is in a common life, and because he bears his brothers' burdens. And so in all the efforts of the Church. As it sings its songs, they are the songs of united brethren. As it preaches, as it resolves, as it works, this is not merely for the salvation or blessedness of any individual : it is for the coming in of the kingdom of God, which is the salvation and blessedness of the whole.

2. From another direction, the brotherhood of mankind, or the life in common, is attacked by the Roman Catholic Church. So long as that church exists under its present organization, it exists in defiance of this central tenet of the Christian system. For better, for worse, the centre of the administration of the Christian Church, which never should have had any centre, came to be established at Rome. Rome was the city where, for a thousand years, the theory of government by a head, of obedience below to direction above,

had been carried out. The Emperor of Rome appointed pro-consuls, and prefects who appointed their subordinates, who appointed theirs. And so the world was ruled. If ever there were a system unlike Christ's system, in which men bear each other's burdens, it was that old system of that empire, in which an emperor made the plans, which a proconsul or other officer proclaimed, and the obedient people of the farthest provinces carried through. Well, for better, for worse, I say, that system was copied into the system of what men call the Church of Christ. For the Roman Catholic Church established itself in the city of Rome, and, not unnaturally, took up the methods of administration which it found in civil government. You know what came of that trial. From one end of the world to the other, every Roman Catholic is directed by some superior as to what he shall think, what he shall read, how he shall pray, what he shall do. This superior is himself the inferior of another, that other himself obeys some higher power, and so, link after link of a chain, they all depend on the one central power of Rome, which is at the head of all. Thus, in one system and by one direction, the faithful Roman Catholic is told on what days he shall eat fish, and on what he shall eat eggs; that he may not read John Milton, and that he may read Mr. Malleck's meanness and vulgarity. He is told that he shall do this, and shall not do that; and under such tutelage inevitably loses sight of that mutual work of man with man and brother with brother which Jesus Christ proposed, and on which rests his kingdom. Contrast the ideal fulfilment of the Roman Catholic system of obedience as carried out in one of the Jesuit colonies of Paraguay or of California, so highly extolled by the Roman authors,— contrast that against the work of a congregational democracy. Such a democracy was the system of Paul, and of the rest, for three hundred years before this other system of hierarchies and obedience was so much as tried in the Church. It compelled every one to bear his brother's burdens. It was not afraid of the most exalted language of that book which is crowded most full of the most exalted language of the most poetic inspiration. It was not afraid to say to those humblest in earthly condition, "Ye are all kings and priests." Of such a system the administration, from the nature of things, works its way into every fibre of the common life. But of the Roman Catholic system, any man who sees it here would say that it is foreign to the mutual life of our New England towns, because they are founded on the prin-

ciple of the life in common. I always look on the proced-
ures of the Roman Church in our villages as I might look on
a bit of middle-age armor, or the shield and spear of some
Fiji warrior in the house of a friend. It is an imported curiosity, which has nothing to do with the life with which it is
surrounded. It is foreign. I should willingly leave this to
the decision of any conscientious priest of that faith. I do
not see one here. I wish I did. I would gladly ask him if
he do not feel that he and his are strangers in this common
life of one of our towns. I think he would acknowledge it,
and that he would say that the Roman system meant such
strangeness. His vows exclude him from a personal knowledge of family life. His obligation of obedience to his supe-
riors is such that if they order him to-night to go to Australia, with the light of morning to Australia he must go. It
is not meant that his life should be rooted in with the life of
the people. It is meant that it shall not be. Because of
this, it necessarily happens that the worship of that church is
one thing and the life of the community is another. Thus:
it has nothing to do with the reading-rooms, with the public
library, with social amusement, with arrangements for public
improvement. It withdraws from co-operation in charities, it
keeps aloof intentionally from all the common life of the
community, because it is based, not on the principle of
mutual help of brethren, but on the principle of hierarchies
of service and of obedience of inferiors. But that congregational system in which the Church of Christ throve for three
centuries before this Roman system was thought of, taught
and teaches each one that he is intrusted with power to be
used for the benefit of all.

Here is the difference between the missions of the congregational church and those missions which the Jesuit brotherhood sends out to call to obedience to its general the savages
on the other side of the world. For instance, in these mountains, here is a gore which has been left by the surveyor between two townships in the wilderness ; and you hear that one
or two squatters have straggled in there, and that their children are growing up, if we dared say so, without God in the
world. Who is to be the missionary to this people? The
congregational system answers, " He or she, be it boy or girl,
be it man or woman, who lives nearest to them, who has ever
read a chapter of the gospel, or who has ever been taught to
repeat the Lord's Prayer." Or they tell you of the Western
wilderness, and of the wild frontiersmen who govern there.

" Have you any priest there to give the sacrament or to offer prayer ? " To be sure we have a priest there ; we have a thousand priests there in the congregational system. Every child of God who has received any life or any light from this gospel as it extends itself, is priest and king in proportion as he has so received. It is for him to give to others of the treasure which has been given to him. It is his business to bear his brothers' burdens.

It is from this mutual principle, and because it is committed to this mutual principle, that the Liberal Church is the only church possible for a republic ; and I may reverse the language and say that a republic is only possible where the Church is working in liberal ways. Dr. Furness says, in one of his unpublished discourses, that no theological writer, trained under the habits of absolute governments, has as yet appeared to understand what Jesus Christ meant by "The Kingdom of Heaven." The analogy with the methods of an earthly kingdom is in itself always deceptive, as the Saviour himself was forever showing. This King, who is to reign over this heavenly kingdom,— why, he is our Father. In this kingdom, all we are · brethren. Here is no such king as Herod, as Antiochus, as Tiberius, as Augustus. The mere suggestion is almost blasphemy. So far the Christian Church everywhere would assent to me. What the Church does not understand in absolute governments is, that a kingdom of brethren ruled over by a Father is in no sort like a kingdom of prefects and proconsuls,— of lord-lieutenants and major-generals commanding,— though ruled over by a Victor Emanuel, a Frederic William, or a Napoleon III. It knows nothing of their iron castes and graded hierarchies. The kingdom of heaven, as Jesus Christ and as Paul speak of it, is the Christian commonwealth, as Milton and Winthrop and Samuel Adams have conceived of it. They could not express their dreams for the State in simpler words, or words more practical, than the Master used, or than those which Paul put down in epigram, when he said,—
"Bear ye one another's burdens ; this is the whole law of Christ."
As against Calvinists, on the one hand,— who in their eagerness to save souls are magnifying individualism with all its dangers,— the Liberal Church has to exhort them to save the world of which they are. She has to root out selfishness, even in that form where religiosity has consecrated it and

petted it. On the other side,— against the Catholic Church and its imitators, against all the little popes and little conclaves, which profess that certain rulers are to direct and that we subjects are to follow,— the Liberal Church is to proclaim that we are all brethren. "Brethren in the Life in Common" was the noble name which some of those Protestants before the Reformation chose in the Middle Ages,— a name too good to be forgotten.

From this principle spring all leagues and societies and unions that are worth the name. From this principle in modern history have sprung all those confederations which have bound separate tribes together. All United States, all United Empires, belong to this gradual extension of the Christian principle. This nation of ours, whose very motto might be said to be taken from the discourse at the last supper, so truly is she one made out of many, is an illustration of the triumph of the Christian principle. It is in the admission of this principle that the prophecy shall be fulfilled, in which nation shall not take arms against nation, neither shall men study war any more.

IV. But I do not choose that you young people shall say that this is no matter for you, that you are not yet engaged in these matters of social organization, and that such illustrations of statesmanship do not enter into your lives. You can see the same thing in these very surroundings in which we live to-day. Our friend from Salem described it yesterday as he contrasted the two passengers who entered the same railway car, one of them governed by the selfish spirit and the other living in the common life.

Compare two people in a mountain hotel this summer. Claudia comes in from her lonely walk, and passes across the crowded piazza to her room, with the specimens she is to analyze and press, with the rhyme ready for her new sonnet, and the thoughts ready for her old diary,— retiring there unloved, unhonored, unknown. Compare her, I say, against Mary, who took with her a dozen school-girls and school-boys on her walk, and has started these on watching the growth of the lichens, those on making a trophy of mushrooms, another set on writing a ballad of the saw-mill, and brings them back a rollicking, cheerful company, all bearing each other's burdens,— who can hardly let her slip out of their sight, and are, all the same, eager to forward her every wish and to relieve her in every anxiety. I do not say, Compare the stiff, three-page entry in Claudia's diary with Mary's cool indifference to any record of a happy day. I do not say which of those two girls is the more joyful in the life she has chosen. That is not what I am after. I do say that that experiment once fairly tried by the girl who chooses the larger life instead of the smaller,— life in God's way instead of life alone,— will show her so thoroughly what the life in common is,— the life more abundant,— that she will be in little danger of sinking back on life separate, life petty, life tied to her own digestion, her own headaches, or her own "culture." She learns what was meant as long ago as the Apostles' Creed by, "I believe in the Holy Church Universal."

V. The principle of the life in common is now far assumed that in our time almost every man is willing to hold to it a certain allegiance. In some insignificant way, men will attempt to pick up some of its pebbles though they are not bold enough to trust to its open ocean. Thus one man asks you to become an Odd Fellow,— which is a very good thing ; or another urges you to become a Freemason,— which is a very good thing ; another proposes that you shall be a Knight of Pythias, another that you shall join an engine company. You know it is said that in those times of Trajan, to which our friend alluded yesterday, the only organization in which man was permitted to join with man in the Roman Empire was in the organization of the fire department, where necessity overruled the selfishness of the Roman law because they had to permit men to unite, when they "ran with the machine." Why, they will even ask you to join a burying society, though that always seemed to me a somewhat grim and grisly form of the principle of universal life. For the man to attend a meeting, feeling that to obtain the fullest profit from it he must hope that it is the last meeting he will ever attend, seems the very minimum of the principle on which all meetings are held. But each of these is only a partial illustration. There are organizations at hand where it is quite possible for men to assert the whole principle and take the whole benefit of the life in common. They are simple, but they do exhibit, in one detail or in another detail, all that might be and can be when the Christian congregation or the Christian Church asserts to the full the powers of sympathy and union. As we heard this morning the repetition of the eternal thrilling cry, "What is the voice of the Spirit" to the churches of New Hampshire? I could not but feel that the practical answer is, that we establish more churches. I do not care if only a dozen persons are knit together in such an organization. Suppose they begin by singing hymns together. Suppose they agree to teach each other's children. Suppose they lend a hand, each with each, in the lifting up the social life of the town in which they are. Suppose they meet together to read and to listen to reading. Let this little congregation, though there were in it but a dozen persons, men, women, and children, meet often and regularly for the common services of worship in common, let it enter into the mutual charities of neighbors and friends, let it determine to lift to a higher plane, and so to enlarge the life, of all who live in that region, and it finds out the blessing and strength of mutual life.

To carry out such enterprises the better, we form such light organizations, quite without hamper and friction, as these which unite the congregations of the Liberal Church. That church enters upon its perfect work, as by its missions, in its publications, by its schools, and in such united worship as we are maintaining here, it reveals to men the infinite strength of mutual service, the comfort and the victory of

"THE LIFE IN COMMON."

ᐸ//ᴧ

BODY, MIND, AND SOUL.

A SERMON

PREACHED AT THE SOUTH CONGREGATIONAL CHURCH,

MAY 25, 1879,

BY

REV. EDWARD E. HALE.

BOSTON:

GEO. H. ELLIS, PRINTER, 101 MILK STREET.

1879.

BODY, MIND, AND SOUL.

It is a month ago to-day that I bade good-bye to the winter section of our vesper congregation. Boston is itself a university now. Thousands of young men and young women come here to study every winter,— in the musical conservatories, in the schools of design and of painting, in the lecture-rooms,— and other places of instruction; and when the spring opens, they are away to the West, or the South, or the Pacific. The attraction of our vesper service draws in hundreds of such young people every Sunday. I see them, without even knowing their names. They make one of our two congregations. From this home of a winter,— where they light as a bird of passage lights for its winter rest,— they carry to homes far away such glad tidings as they have heard here, whether quickened by the melody of Mendelssohn or by the intensity of Isaiah. For me, I know their faces, perhaps, but not their names. Only I know that when May is ended they are gone, and that probably they will never see me again, nor I them. A farewell to them, therefore, is a real farewell,— with little feeling on their part, maybe, but with much on mine; and I tried the other day to give them, in five minutes, the last message of the eternal life which would ever go from me to them.

This incident — or accident, if you choose to call it so — has set me to thinking whether it might not be possible to put in order the winter's last words to you young people of our own congregation, who are not going to Nebraska or California, who are coming back to work and live here. Whether I cannot, to advantage, state with a little system, the plan and purpose on which you ought to be starting on life,— taking more time than five minutes for the laying out of that purpose, and speaking to you with the familiarity of an old friend whom you have seen and heard perhaps ever since you were born. I shall try, in the four sermons before the school vacations emancipate us all, to give some such hints .

of the system of life to young people who are beginning to direct life for themselves. I hope I need not say that the outlook and direction of all that I say shall be purely and simply religious, that it will come out on the supremacy of the soul over flesh and sense, and that the object of all such plan and system shall be the coming nearer to God,— what is called by careful writers " Blessedness." But, though that is the ultimate object, the success of the voyage will not be assured merely by talk of the ultimate object. No man arrives at New Orleans by merely talking about New Orleans, or about levees and cotton-crops, or by drawing pictures of palm-trees and pelicans. If you want to go to New Orleans, the first step is to find the way, the second is to obtain money for the journey, the third is to pack your trunk, and the fourth to buy a ticket for New York. All four of these seem, to a blind observer, very unlike entering New Orleans. All the same, are they the necessary beginning. And we — while we are to remember that oneness with God in life and purpose is the great object of a child of God — must not so befog ourselves or bedrug ourselves, as to fail to take in order our initial steps, however commonplace they may seem,— even carnal or temporal. We are infinite spirits. Yes ! But we are in finite bodies. And the school God has been pleased to place us in, is the school where we are to train those infinite spirits, by the earthly chalk on the somewhat grimy blackboards of Monday, Tuesday, Wednesday, and the rest, and their respective duties. It may be house-cleaning, it may be book-keeping or other calculation, it may be planing or sawing. If it is honest work, we can make it part of our training for angeldom. And that is just what it is for.

In this business of making ready to achieve the great result we seek, the matter of prime interest and importance is to learn our own place and our own power. How much can we do, and where must we stop? We are children of God ; yes. But we are not God ; no. This is to say, we may have infinite longings, infinite desires, but we cannot achieve everything ; we are not omnipotent. And the first lesson is to learn what the limitations are, that we may not waste zeal and force. Who wants to kick against the pricks ?

I am sorry to say that the pulpit is not always helpful in this direction, nor are the other enterprises which clergymen direct. Because it is their business to show the infinite powers which you hold, they may be apt not to acknowledge

fairly the difficulties which surround you ; and the discourage-
ments which set in sometimes on conscientious young people
belong largely to this failure of ours. Be that as it may, I
will try to avoid this mistake now. I begin by saying
squarely that you cannot do at once everything that you would
like to do, or that I should like to have you do ; or, which is
a much better way to put it, you cannot do at once what God
himself would like to have you do, and what he begs you to do
some day. You cannot go to New Orleans in an instant, nor
without passing over the space between, nor without getting
ready. You can go in five days ; while many a man, doing
his best, has been five months. The day may come when
you can go in five hours. When you are an angel, you may
go in no time. But while you are man or human, that is not
possible,— while you are girt with human conditions of time
and space. We will accept these conditions ; we will accept
the inevitable ; we will not kick against the pricks ; we will
not make as good resolutions as we can ; we will only resolve
on what men and women, boys and girls, youths and maidens,
can perform.

Speaking, then, to and for such young men and young
women, just as they leave school and as they assert the
rights and take the privileges of self-control, my advice to
them — precisely because they are at what has been called
the omnipotent age — is, not to attempt omnipotence. At
the best, you are under many limitations, and it is best you
should be. You boys and young men are to be in stores or
offices, or in college or other apprenticeship. You girls will
have home duties, not as agreeable, perhaps, as the school
duties were, but none the less binding. Besides these demands, society has demands. You must receive visits and
make them. You must eat and drink ; perhaps you must
prepare your food and arrange the table. You must wear
clothes ; you ought to earn the money which pays for them.
Perhaps it is your place to make them. There are younger
brothers and sisters in the family : it is your place to take a
fair share in the charge of them. Such are a few instances
of the duties and cares which hem you in, which you must not
struggle against. Do not think that, like a boy in a story in a
sixpenny newspaper, you can swing yourself out of a window
by a cord and go off with a parcel on your back, and so be
free of mankind. You are in a world where you are all knit
up with other people. Accept that position once for all, and
do not struggle against it.

Watching life as it is, and striking a rough average of different experiences, I am apt to say to my young friends, who are making their own plans, that, at the beginning, they had better satisfy themselves with marking out the use which they will make of two or three hours a day. As things are, I think that will be as much as they can generally manage well. I mean to say that most young men owe their employers ten hours of the working day. If, beside that, they can manage two hours, whether in the evening, or, in this season, in the early morning, for their own uses, I think they should be satisfied. Only crowd these hours full. The same is true of young women who are engaged in shops, in offices, or in other regular vocations away from home. And, to continue to speak with the same precision, young women who are at home without a profession, calling, or vocation will have domestic duties such as I alluded to, and social calls, which are duties also,— so frequent, and making such demands on vital powers, that they had better not make plans, as I believe, for more than three hours in a day. The young woman who fights for more, fights at disadvantage: she has not her work well in hand, and is constantly worried and worn. The apparent difference between the two hours' people and the three hours' people, as I have divided them, is not, in fact, real. There are certain advantages which belong to the first class, as I think we shall see.

I am also in the habit of saying, in a very mechanical and wooden way, if you please, when I offer advice as to the use of these hours : —

Divide them between body, mind, and soul, and, if you are at all afraid of a mistake, divide them evenly. Take an hour for bodily exercise; take an hour for the training of your mind ; and also one hour in such work for others, such talk with God, or for both, that you may be more manly and more womanly — more like Him — when the day has gone by. The counsel is sufficiently wooden to be remembered. In practice, of course, it can be deviated from in detail. Of course, the three uses of time may all be subserved at once. All the same it is true, that each day, and the part of it for which you are responsible, ought to see you advance in the training of body, mind, and soul.

Now, with regard to the first of these, those of you who have had to walk to an office or a shop in the morning and back at night, have managed your physical exercise by the way. You have, then, your two hours free for the intellectual training you seek, and for your unselfish duties; and that is all that, under our plan, those persons are to devote to these cares who have no stated vocation which calls them out of doors.

Mechanical as this subdivision seems, I have found it, in a thousand cases, convenient to make it, relying, of course, on good-sense and good-feeling to interpret and administer the rule. Nor have I ever known, whether in written biography or in the experience of others confided to me, a case of disordered life, or of low spirits, which are the signs of disordered life, which could not be improved by a fair administration of a rule so simple, even if it be wooden. Low spirits are the sign that something is wrong. When your patient finds that he is in protracted low spirits, make him tell whether, in his management of a day, he does not neglect his bodily exercise, or his mental training, or that unselfish life — that life for God and man — which a man's soul requires.

In such an attack of depressed spirits, it has become now almost a commonplace to say at once that the patient probably needs physical exercise, and so to send him out to row in a boat, to take a walk, or to ride on horseback. Here is a crude recognition of the necessity involved. But it is not certain that the deficiency is the need of physical exercise. There are men and women who have exercise enough in the open air who know, only too well, what are the terrors of depressed spirits. The danger is the danger of any want of balance. That man knows it who is caring only for his physical exercise; that man knows it who is caring only for his books and intellectual training; and, alas, many a man and many a woman have known it who have devoted all their powers only to religious aspirations. In such cases, what I have a right to call a moral dyspepsia, results as certainly and terribly as ever physical dyspepsia under one of the other exaggerations. Poor Cowper's hymns, written under just such experience, are terrible instances.

> "My soul is sad and much dismayed;
> See, Lord, what legions of my foes,
> With fierce Apollyon at their head,
> My heavenly pilgrimage oppose!
> See from the ever-burning lake
> How like a smoky cloud they rise!
> With horrid blasts my soul they shake,—
> With storms of blasphemies and lies.

> "Their fiery arrows reach the mark,
> My throbbing heart with anguish tear;
> Each lights upon a kindred spark
> And finds abundant fuel there."

You young people hardly know that there are such expressions in literature. For that, you may thank your training in a Unitarian church. But that is what the best men have felt,— nay, have thought it their duty to feel. And to-day, whoever undertakes to train himself only on the side of religious emotion — whoever says, "Nearer, my God, to thee," and says that only, without seeing that it involves care for this body God made and this mind which God would use — comes out upon that sad gloom only one step this side insanity. And I declare to you, that when people come to a clergyman for religious advice and instruction, nine times out of ten here is their difficulty. It is not that they have thought too little upon the written record of religion or its external services, but that they have thought too much of them. Just as the doctor finds the dyspeptic is thinking too much of his appetite, just so the clergyman finds his moral dyspeptic thinking too much of his soul and its repentances. Just as the skilful doctor sends his dyspeptic away to Texas or to Europe,— because he knows the amusement and occupation of a new land will divert him, without his knowing it, from that morbid counting of his own pulse and talk about his own appetite,— so the great Physician, the Curer of souls, treats his patients. He does not talk over the case with his Mary Magdalene, or with his other penitents. He sets them to work. He sends one to this duty, and one to that. Two and two, he sends them all over Galilee. "See what I am doing: do that. See how white the harvest is: go reap." It is all summed up in one direction. They forget themselves because they follow him. And to-day, nine times in ten, to the pale, nervous, weeping, anxious penitent, who comes into a minister's study for guidance, who says he cannot pray, he does not enjoy the church, he is afraid he is an infidel, he cannot make the ninety-ninth verse of the fifty-fourth chapter of this Prophecy agree with the second verse of the third chapter of that Gospel,— to such a moral dyspeptic the duty of his adviser is to say, "Dear friend, you have been making, not too little of formal religion, but too much of it." And his skill is shown if, by example, by philosophy, by tender leading by the hand, he can break up that maladministration of life, and

more wisely divide into mutual and complementary services
the opportunities of the time which God has given.

Now it will be my business to show to you young people,
in the next three Sundays, first, that this physical exercise —
which Paul says is so profitable — plays right into the formation of the perfect manhood and womanhood which we expect
from you ;
To show again, on another Sunday, that every day you
must do something in the line of mental training, and that
this also can and shall contribute to life eternal ;
And to show, third, how all this — how the work of your
vocation or your avocation — may and must be lighted up with
the infinite glory,— the work, not of machines, not of creatures of God's intelligence, but of the living and eternal children of God's love,— those who are life from his life, sparks
from his fire,— of him, from him, and to him always. I will
not, then, speak of these details to-day. To-day,— if I should
never see you again nor you me, if you were going as those
vesper boys and girls have gone,— what I would say is
this : —
Body, soul, and spirit, offer yourselves wholly, joyfully, and
simply to your God. This is to say, do not separate your
religion from the rest of life, but soak your life in your religion and your religion in your life ; for you ought not to be
able to separate the two. You are not God's child on
Sunday, and a child of the world on Monday. You are
God's child all the time. It is not God's law that you obey
when you eat the bread of communion, and the world's law
when you compute interest in the counting-room. It is all
God's law, and you can make the one duty as sacred as the
other. You can row your boat, when you are pulling in a
match, loyally, bravely, truly, as a pure, unselfish boy rows it,
and so as to please God who gives you strength for that endeavor. You can sit at the piano and practise your scales,
humbly, patiently, and with the same determination with
which an archangel goes about his duties. You can do that
to God's glory. And God is pleased when you make that
endeavor. You can take the baby to ride, you can lift his
carriage upon the curb-stone gently when there is a street to
cross, you can meet the perplexities and irritations of that
care, as Uriel stood before the sun to keep watch and ward.
The charge may be as true, as pure, and as grand. It may
be a part of your sacrifice and of your religion.

For you and me, the effort is to be, not simply to stand at the altar, or to watch the wreaths of incense, or to repeat simply the words of the service,— though this in its place may please us and help us,— but to make the world a temple as we make life a joy, by living, moving, and being in God, with God, and for God. I have not chosen to speak of your summer-vacation life alone. I am quite as earnest about your lives of daily routine. That common care may be glorified, that daily duty may be made divine to you,— this is the beginning, middle, and end. The Word is very nigh us, if only we will hear, and see, and remember, and obey.

From May to November.

A second series of sermons preached by Mr. Hale in the South Congregational Church will be published weekly. After the 6th of September, each sermon will usually be published the Saturday after it is preached.

But the first sermon of this series was

THE LIFE IN COMMON,

preached by Mr. Hale before the New Hampshire Conference, at its meeting at Weir's Landing.

The next sermon of this series will be "Bodily Training."

These sermons are published by GEO. H. ELLIS, 101 Milk Street. Price, 10 cents each, or $1.00 for the series of fifteen.

BODILY TRAINING.

A SERMON

PREACHED AT THE SOUTH CONGREGATIONAL CHURCH,

BOSTON,

BY

EDWARD E. HALE.

BOSTON:

GEO. H. ELLIS, PRINTER, 101 MILK STREET.

1879.

BODILY TRAINING.

—— —— ——

God's temple is holy,— which temple ye are.— I. Cor. iii., 17.

I am to speak to-day, as I promised last Sunday, on the part which physical exercise takes in the highest training of young people.

It was my duty nine years ago to deliver a course of lectures at the Lowell Institute, on the Divine Method of Human Life. I began then, as I do now, on the physical exercises of manhood or womanhood. Early in the autumn, to my great pleasure but equal surprise, I received a letter from a stranger, who wrote, he said, to thank me for those lectures. When we came to the detail of his thanks, it was not that I had quickened him in prayer; it was not that he had more hope of heaven or more tender love for his family, though I had tried for all these things; it was not that he had tried the course I suggested for the improvement of his memory, his imagination, or his logical powers. No! I was left to guess whether I had helped him there. The good that I had done was that I had made him swim, almost every day, in what he called "the South Boston sea." "When I do not," he said, "like the Roman, I have lost a day; and, when I do, I think of you, and bless you for making me exercise." So, as late as the 2d of November, he wrote to thank me for his bath of the 31st of October in the "deep, lone sea."

I tell that story as a fair enough illustration of the way in which we may all start out of the ruts which by chance we are rolling in, and because I hope it may suggest to others the question whether they are using to the full — were it for pleasure only — this wonderful machine, the body, the organ most perfect of all, of which Paul and the other masters say things as wonderful as in this text. We have passed well beyond that horrible abuse of the body which the monks and other ascetics favored. Augustine called it "load and lumber." "When will it please God to give me 'leave to lay down this load and lumber of the flesh?'"

And, for fourteen hundred years, most of the religious writers of the Church echoed those blasphemies. This is the more curious, and one almost says the more wicked, because the New Testament really contains, in one place and another, a very good little code of physical exercise; and Paul, in his poetical way, speaks, as we have seen, in the most intense words of the dignity of the human body, its excellence and its beauty. With the decline of mere clerical domination, such central truths reassert themselves, and almost everybody now sees just what Paul says and Jesus implies: that if we are to serve God well we must use good tools. One of these tools is the body; and the keen, quick, and proper use of all the senses and all the organs becomes, not simply a human convenience or a finite accomplishment, but the measure of our eagerness to enter into God's service, as it is the measure of the work we can do in bringing forward God's kingdom. Say, if you please, that the faithful coal-heaver serves God in his faithfulness, and that Ambrose does no more when he sings " Te Deum." Still there is not one of us who would not rather sing " Te Deum" than heave coal; and the moment it is clear that by my faithful training of my body I can pass from the service which a brute could render to the service of an angel, so soon my obligation to do so comes in. Just what I am here for, is that, day by day and week by week, my service may be nobler and better, until at last I am clothed upon with my house which is from heaven,— till I use new powers and new senses in service yet higher. Nay, even then, the enlargement of power, or what the Scripture calls "growth in grace," is the law without end of a child of God.

I have said already that whatever the measure of care boy or girl may give to gratify his spiritual aspirations and yearnings, and whatever the measure of care or of time he may give to the training of intellectual faculties, as much care and as much time must be given to physical exercise. And it must be given every day. It does not answer to spend two months at the Adirondacks in vigorous out-door exercise, then two months at school in crowding all steam to pass a competitive examination, with the idea that then one can go through a series of camp-meetings or anniversary weeks, or other protracted religious exercises, and so, as my German friend said, square the account for one's soul for a year. There is a good deal of this pushing things through, as if to get them out of the way : indeed, it is said to be an American passion; but it is all wrong. The vital power, whatever those words mean, of each single day, is to be fairly distributed each day between body, mind, and soul. And, to take again the hint, of which I spoke last week, which is given by a fit of low spirits, you will find, almost infallibly, that such an invasion comes on, when you have been steadily neglecting one or two of these three sides of your triple life. Your physical exercise has run behindhand,— or your mental training has run behindhand,— or the growth of your affections, of your immortal soul, has run behindhand. As we live, in a social condition curiously intricate, the fault is quite as likely to be the first of these as either of the other two.

You will not expect me to go into those details which you would find in a book of athletic training, or in any of the hand-books of accomplishments. But I will say, frankly, that I believe the pulpit would be better occupied in square, didactic instructions as to such detail than it is in much of its merely ecclesiastical suggestions. I will speak now very briefly — with the brevity indeed of a catalogue — of the more important of these specific duties, and will trust that my young friends will themselves work out the detail. Our chief business to-day is to drag them up from the class of indifferent things, and place them once for all in the class of essential and absolute necessities. We are to lift them from the list of what Miss Edgeworth called the "May haves" up to the list of what she called the "Must haves." That is to say,— because we mean to have in the end a perfect mind and a perfect soul, and nothing less, we will strive in the beginning, as far as lies in us, for a perfect body and nothing less.

To begin with, then, the duty of sleep, profound and healthy, is the first of the physical duties,— good sleep and enough sleep. Whatever hinders it must be thrown overboard. Even the old proverbs must give way, if need be,— the requisite in young life being that you shall rise for a day's duty hopeful, cheerful, and strong, with none of yesterday's arrears to carry. Do not forget the gospel direction, that you are to be new-born every morning, and to start, really with the freshness of a little child. If your fit of special exertion yesterday,— the German protracted till two o'clock in the morning, the puzzle in the counting-room to find out where those lost two cents had gone from the balance-sheet,— if such things as these last night bring you to this morning with a hot head, after feverish tossing through the small hours, you are simply committing suicide by inches. And such suicide is not to be judged by different canons than those which condemn the sudden blow.

Sleep comes without asking and without thought, indeed, when we are loyally obeying the great laws; when we are in the service which is perfect freedom. "He giveth his beloved sleep," is an oracle of profound significance.*

Now I know I traverse the habits, and I suppose the opinions, of many excellent people, when I say that exercise in the open air in every-day of life is also a necessity for young people who are well and who would keep well. I know what the excuses are,— of climate, dress, occupation, and all that. Let them go. The truth is that fresh air is health, and the loss of it is disease. Nor is that American habit I ridicule, of trying to do all your work at once and in the bulk, ever more absurd than when we try to take all our fresh air on Monday by an excursion down the harbor, and so to buy the right to live shut up in prison Tuesday, Wednesday, and Thursday, over our dress-making or house-keeping, our accounts or other business, or our study. I am to speak by and by of the nearer communion with God which a man enjoys who walks with him, as Adam did in the garden, in the cool of the day. It is not of that that I speak now, but of the mere physical conditions which keep the physical machine in order. For a person in health, the preservation of health demands daily exercise in the open air, winter or summer, country or city, cold or hot, wet or dry.

And, though I have eschewed detail, let me ask my young friends to undertake it. It is worth any boy's while, or any girl's, for instance, to see what care those old Greeks thought it worth while to give to such matters. Look, for instance, in such books as Anacharsis's Travels, Landor's Pericles and Aspasia, Becker's Charicles, or the proper articles in Smith's Dictionary, to see how it was that the Greek sculptors had at hand such forms as the Apollo, the Genius of Life, or the Venus of Milo. It was by no accident that Sophocles lived strong and well till he was ninety-five,— or that

* Without attempting detail, which, indeed, I have attempted in another place, I ought to say here, perhaps, that hard mental work in the last three or four hours of the waking day is to be avoided. Do not calculate in those hours, do not study any mathematics or other difficult study, and try not to write your letters then. On the other hand, fresh walk in the open air is an excellent preparative for sleep.

the little city of Athens, when it was not as big as Lawrence or Worcester is to-day, had then such a cluster of well-trained men, with bodies well-nigh perfect. These men were trained in a school which sought for bodily health by system and regimen.

If I were to speak of details, it would not be simply the exercises of the Greek gymnasium. I have been asked to say a special word as to the value of sweeping a room as a physical exercise for women or men, and I ought to say that some scientific persons give it the first place. Dancing, also, deserves the place which it has won in all history and in all civilizations, except that of the Puritans; and there, as you know, it has fought its way through, though against tremendous odds. Of course you would not advise a boy to dance all night, more than you would advise a girl to sweep all day; and there ought to be as little danger of one excess as the other. If, again, while I pass other exercises without a word, I select the exercise of swimming, it is because this community is just now neglecting it. Our new sewer will be worth the three million dollars it costs us, if, in truth, we gain from it the clean waters we once had all along the shore. If I had my way, there should be public and universal instruction in swimming, for girls as well as boys. In the event of accident, a woman ought to be as well able as a man to save her own life or to rescue others. I do not think it is creditable to this city that other cities should be far in advance of us, in their provisions for teaching swimming. And it is to be said of swimming that it is an absolutely perfect exercise.

Thus much of those physical exercises which are simply personal, which Robinson Crusoe might and must have followed out on his island, though he were never to be rescued. There is another series which will interest you young people more, because they have to do with your relations with others; although you could carry them out on a desert island, in fact you train yourself in them because we live in society with others. These are the lines of what we call "accomplishments," not speaking very precisely. Here, again, I do not attempt much detail, but I do want you to consider them as moral beings do. I want to put them on the plane of morals. And if you will put them there, you may study the details yourselves. Your consciences, quick and pure, and sustained by God in answer to your prayer, are your oracles, much more quick and reliable for you than any judgments of mine.

8

With regard to some of these accomplishments, the decision is already practically made. For instance, it is taken for granted that all of you, and all decent people, shall know how to write. This is a pure physical exercise; as much so as is fencing or swimming. It is expected, and rightly expected, that everybody shall compass that accomplishment. Now, shall we go a step further. Every one who can write can learn to draw. Shall we insist that they all do? or shall we say that only persons with a distinct artistic genius shall learn? or shall we say that only they shall learn, and, beside them, certain others also who can be of use in teaching drawing?

I am quite clear here, that we are right in exacting the rudiments of this accomplishment from all. I do not believe that you will all be artists; nor is there any reason why you should. But there is every reason why you should represent correctly and not incorrectly what you see and what you mean. There is every reason why, if you give a carpenter directions for repairing your house, you should be able to direct him and not to misdirect him. When the general calls upon you from the ranks some day, sends you out as a scout, and you return with information, you ought to be able to plot it properly on paper. When you discover a new flower, or a new insect in the wilderness, you ought to be able to represent it correctly in the interests of science for those who study. Perhaps your sense of color is dull; perhaps your memory of form is bad. None the less ought you to be able to see, and to put on paper what you see. And the truth is, that learning to draw is learning to see. For the rest, let those who love their drawing keep on with it and go further. Let the others pass it by and take up other exercises. "Those who love it,"—that is a better statement than "those who have a genius for it." If they love it enough to persevere, their genius, more or less, will take care of itself. And this definition is accurate enough for any young scholar to apply it in his own training.

The next question is infallibly as to the training of the voice, still a matter of physical culture. This city says that every child shall try to learn to sing. Is this wise or not wise? Wise, I should say, that they should try; but this also is as I try all soils and only cultivate the rich soils, as I try all stones and only smelt those which prove to be ores. Not but a little music may be a very pleasant thing; still let us not make young people miserable by straining for a faculty which God has not given. When we have tried, let us abide by the trial, nor keep on unless there be reason. This is to be said, however, in connection with what the president of the college said to you young men on Wednesday evening : * You do want to speak in public, and both boys and girls want to read aloud and to read well. The careful training for singing is probably the best exercise for the public speaker, and the present striking deficiency of the home circle — its difficulty in finding good readers — will cease when it has those who have opened their chests, learned to use all their muscles, and given range to the register of voice by exercise in singing.

One step further. We will try all the children in singing, and we will give up those who do not love it or those who cannot learn. Shall we try them all with instruments of music ? Shall we place fifty thousand piano-fortes in the fifty thousand dwelling-houses of Boston ? or, failing them, shall we substitute parlor organs, harps and citherns, violins and instruments of ten strings ? Such seems to be the present disposition, encouraged, as I have sometimes supposed, by the manufacturing disposition of the New Englander, and our skill in making musical instruments of the first quality.

But, as you see, the plan travels beyond the discipline of the man ; it requires that he shall also possess an instrument and a complex instrument. And it is probably at this line that we are to stop. If he love music, let him learn to play; if he love it enough, let him be Joseph Haydn, or Mendelssohn, or Rubinstein. But if he do not love it, let him choose for his vocation, or for his avocation, something which he is made for. There may be instances where, with all his love, he will be slow at learning. That is no matter : he has eternity before him. There may be cases where, with all his love, he will never work out the great achievements, so-called. No matter for that. The peasant who first hummed the air of Auld Lang Syne has given as much pleasure in his day as any monarch of music with the grandest symphony. Nay, some blundering choir to-day, as it stumbles through Lyons or Coronation, if it sing with the spirit, comes nearer the Throne of Grace than the Sistine company, if it be singing only with the understanding. The object with which you learn is not success merely, it is not fame merely, but it is best measured by your love of what you learn. And the question you have

* President Eliot at the anniversary of the Christian Union.

to ask is this: "Shall I to-morrow render service more acceptable than I rendered yesterday?"

Of all such rules of detail the principle is the same. The requisite is health, and health means balance of body, mind, and soul. To Jesus Christ himself, in the midst of that cheerful open-air life of his in Galilee, so glad that it has been called a constant festival, poor John the Baptist sent messengers from his underground prison, just as we look out from our dim man-made prisons upon the glories of the world of God. John asked him what he was doing; and had he forgotten all their plans? To whom Jesus answers quite as much of bodily health as of mental; quite as much of mental health as of the aspirations of the soul: quite as much, but no more, for of these he speaks quite as eagerly as of those. But he cannot separate the one from the other. ·He is engaged in care for all three. "In that same hour," says Luke, in his picturesque way, "he cured many of their infirmities and plagues, and of evil spirits"; body and mind alike were comforted; and the message he sent to John was of such comfort as this, of such health as this, with the other message that the glad tidings of God were taught at the same moment, and with the lesson to John, "Blessed is he that shall not be offended in me." What lesson and suggestion for us, in what we are pleased to call our "spiritual experiences"! How far is my hardness of heart, or the melancholy with which I look back on my wicked life,— how far is it a spiritual experience? How much of it is due to disordered digestion? or where do the freaks of a wayward mind, say of a wild imagination or of ill-ordered logic, come in? Or, if I set myself to minister to the poor, as he did, how certain it is that I must prepare myself, not simply with the Bible which I carry to read to the sick, but with the good sense which shall answer the cross-questioning of the dissatisfied, and also with the gospel of cleanliness and the open air with which I am to dispel head-ache and heart-ache together. The whole lesson of Jesus Christ is thus for balance,— for that health which is the balance of training with training, and faculty upon faculty. And when we ask these young friends of ours to make him the leader of their lives, this is what we mean,— that in all such directions as we have been tracing he shall be master. He knew how to live, knew how to extort the most from life, to make it abundant, to make it glad, and to

make it useful. And you, when you try to give to these physical exercises some sense, some moderation, some purpose
and meaning, whether it be in a running-match, or whether
it be in practising the scale, you are not on the right track
unless the unity of all life appears to you, as he showed it.
You are not training your voice or your hand or your foot or
your eye for your own behoof alone : it is that you may bear
your brother's burden the better. Who does this fulfils
Christ's whole law. And, because he fulfils it, he does more
than appears to the eye. While he trains the body, he trains
mind and soul. The obedience which compels these fingers
to that distasteful task, as they pass up and down the keys, is
the same quality of life with which Gabriel bears God's message from one end of heaven to the other. The steadiness
which holds to its purpose till the last moment of the foot-
race is the endurance which endures to the end, of which
endurance, safety, or salvation, is the reward. Such unity and
harmony of exercise and of life are the blessing of him or of
her who chooses the Lord of Life for a personal leader.

From May to November.

A second series of sermons preached by Mr. Hale in the South Congregational Church will be published weekly. After the 6th of September, each sermon will usually be published the Saturday after it is preached.

The sermons already published are—

> THE LIFE IN COMMON,
> BODY, MIND, AND SOUL,
> BODILY TRAINING.

These sermons are published by GEO. H. ELLIS, 101 Milk Street. Price, 10 cents each, or $1.00 for the series of fifteen.

MENTAL DISCIPLINE.

A SERMON

PREACHED AT THE SOUTH CONGREGATIONAL CHURCH,

BOSTON,

BY

EDWARD E. HALE.

BOSTON:

GEO. H. ELLIS, PRINTER, 101 MILK STREET.

1879.

MENTAL DISCIPLINE.

Not to think of himself more highly than he ought to think, but to think soberly.—ROM. xii., 13.

I am to speak to-day of that regular training of mental faculty which, as I claim, is a daily duty for every young man and young woman, and makes a part of the day's exercise. I do not forget for a moment, the contempt with which I have always spoken here, of that canting demand for "culture" which has made that dreadful word ridiculous for a circle of a thousand miles around this city. If anybody ought to know the absurdity of such cant, it is we, who have lived and moved and had our being in the midst of it. I think there is no danger but we shall be on our guard. We are not proposing to sit in easy chairs, and, by lifting boldly at the arms of the chair, to raise ourselves to the heavens. We are not proposing, by any course of primary-school or secondary-school education, to introduce the kingdom of God through the spelling-book. In such follies this community tried its experiments forty years ago. We are hoping to serve God, and to serve him well. We are seeking his kingdom, and would gladly make the entrance to it easier for those who seek to enter. Seeking this, we would get the best use we can of our tools,—tools which he has given us. Nor can a better illustration be found for the training we give the mind—which is one of those tools—than we have had already in the training we should like to give to the body, which is the other.

1. I am to speak first in the way of caution. This caution is to be borne in mind, that mere reading is not, in itself, mental training. There is, in this direction, a popular superstition. But, in truth, the reading of a low-lived novel is as bad training as intimacy with a low-lived man. That every one sees. We may go much farther. To read gossiping novels all day long, is no more mental training than to talk with gossiping fools all day long. It is necessary to give

this caution in advance, because we have but little time in any day in this plan of life which we are following, and we must be careful that that time really goes for what we pretend. We will not deceive ourselves. We will not talk as if reading the newspapers, or reading magazines, or reading novels, did us any great good, or were a part of our training. I hope they will do us no harm ; nor need they. But when we speak of giving an hour a day to mental improvement, we do not speak of this galloping over pages of novels, or columns of newspapers, merely for the entertainment of the hour.

2. If you can arrange among yourselves to work together, a great point is gained. Then the God-given stimulus comes in, in the stimulus of society. These little clubs to read French, to study history, to try experiments in chemistry, to botanize together, or to follow whatever study, are the best possible helps or methods. I never tire of describing the system which they have arrived at at the English Cambridge, after near one thousand years of experiment, as the best possible way of study. The young men, who are studying for honors, make such appointment with their tutors, that each one has every day an hour with his tutor alone. If need be, they study the lesson together. The teacher not only teaches the lesson, but he shows the others how to learn the lesson. Then each scholar works upon the tasks assigned, for two or three hours. And the work of each day ends when all of these teachers and pupils, at the most not more than four, meet with him for an hour, and all together work with mutual help. That is the best system which the experience of so many centuries has devised for the best training for the best men in it.

Now, there is no necessity of going to a university for what is the most valuable part of this training. Its value comes from their all working together. Any three or four friends who can meet daily, or not so often, to read together, can command it. Life quickens life. There is one funny person, one imaginative person, one with a strong memory, one who is steady-going and holds the others to their tasks. The work is of better quality — it is better remembered — and a real training of the mind is involved. It is a great thing to learn to tell what you know. It is a much greater thing to learn to confess ignorance. It is greater yet to learn how to live with others,— how to repress your own arrogance, how to endure other people's ; or, in general, h to make allowance for the finite or fallible elements in other lives, and how to make out, and make the best of, the infinite elements, which are invaluable. All this mental practice is better gained in a literary club, or a circle to read French, than in the City Council or in Congress ; and that is true,—which is always true,—that he who succeeds in these lesser things carries in his success the power to rule cities, as the parable puts it. The experience of the little gives the victory on the larger scale.

3. And what are you to study or to read? On what bone are you to gnaw in this discipline ? The choice is your own. That is the first thing to say. At school you were to do what they told you to do. Now, you are to do what you think you need most and can do best. These two directions go together. You are not always, as a matter of course, to study the thing which you know least. Perhaps, with all the study in the world, you would not compass it. By the time you leave school, you ought to know. Study what you need most and can do best. There is wide range for choice ; but now it is range where your likings and your genius both have play.

Mr. Emerson, who is one of the wisest teachers here, says in one place, when he is directing us how to buy books, that we are to buy books "in the line of our genius." But, for boy or girl of seventeen years of age, the trouble generally ·is, that they do not yet know what the line of their genius is. Nor is it any blame to man or woman, if he cannot, till he die, decide a question so delicate. Mr. Emerson said again, when consulted as to a course of study : "It does not matter so much what you study as with whom you study." Something you are interested in, something you like, and something you need. When one has rightly learned his own ignorance,— and that is what we go to school for,— he ought to be able to choose. If you have found out at seventeen that you cannot well follow the mathematics, leave them for those who can. If, after fair trial, you make nothing of metaphysics, let them go to those who can. If it prove that you delight in the high-ways and by-ways of history,— if. old times begin to grow real to you, and these dead skeletons of names to take flesh and color,— study history. If you follow Stanley, or Kane, or these new travellers in Australia, step by step, with eager curiosity, study geography. If you have won a triumph at the debating club, because you have un-tangled some knot of finance or of tariff, and if the researches of the economist attract you, study real politics,— the economies of wealth. You ought to be able to decide the subject better than any one can choose for you.

4. When you have decided, hold to your decision. I had a young friend who used to come to me once a week, one winter, to borrow books and consult about his reading. At first, I was delighted with the breadth' of his views and the courage of his study. But when I found that, in twenty weeks, he had attacked as many of the fundamental subjects, and abandoned them, I became uneasy. His enthusiasm turned in two months from organic chemistry to Roman jurisprudence, from that to organized philanthropy in modern life, from that to Darwinism and the law of selection, from that to the English Constitution, from that to Augustinianism and the theology of the fall of man, and so on. What made this alarming was, that on each subject he was sure, on successive Saturdays, that it was the only subject for a man of conscience to engage in in our times, and he generally borrowed as many books as he could carry for its study. "Unstable as water, thou shalt not excel." That is the old Hebrew warning against such foolery. Choose your line of study, and hold on; let book lead to book, subject open from subject. Never fear but the range will be wide enough before you have done. I sincerely believe that, with the resources of our great public libraries, any man or woman of spirit who chose to take up a subject of detail, which had not been already wrought out by a specialist, might, in a month's time, be in advance of any person in the community on that line of research. I could safely, I believe, make the statement for a shorter period. You do have the encouragement of feeling that what you work upon may soon be of use to others also. It is not mere "culture." It is work of real service to God and to man. But this implies continued service ; that you shall not fling away week after week of life, like the weather-cock fool I have been describing. Advance from step to step. Make your base here for a movement there ; establish another base for a farther movement ; and never be satisfied to regard the work you are doing as anything less than a part of your contribution eventually to the improvement of the world.

5. If you so regard it, this regular exercise will not be set aside on whatever excuse or fancy. You and your companions will hold to it day by day as indeed a duty, not a bit ˉ relaxation or entertainment merely. You will come to

regard it as something which must be, not to be set aside for
light cause,— more than your dinner, your breakfast, or your
sleep. No harm if in time you make other people regard it
as a necessity. In all new countries, everything is exceptional and nothing regular. I cannot have my meals as
punctually when I have to shoot the rabbit or the deer, and
skin him and cook him for myself, as I can have them when
they are served at a hotel. But the word "civilization"
means escape from such disorder and irregularity. High
civilization means that the ball falls and the bell strikes precisely at twelve ; that the train for New York leaves precisely
at ten or at eight ; that the schools open precisely at nine.
It means as well that when you have seriously agreed with a
circle of your friends to meet regularly at a certain time for
the reading of history, you will do so. That is one of the
things where you will be master. You are not claiming, as
we have seen, to be master for four and twenty hours. For a
great part of the four and twenty hours, you have even
agreed to be obedient to the wishes of others. But for these
two or three hours, you are to be master. Neither your in-
dolence, nor your modesty, nor your good nature, is to sur-
render this claim. Nor are you claiming this for yourself.
As God's child, you are trying to serve him ; and the claim
you make is on his behalf: it is not yours. Having determined, perhaps with others, to follow this course of training
whatever it may be, let that determination be final and
absolute.

Since I have been old enough to have a right to advise my
juniors, placed as I am where it is sometimes my duty to do
so, I have given no piece of counsel of the wisdom of which
I am so sure as of this direction when given to young mothers, engaged at once in the countless difficulties of housekeep-
ing and the charge of young children : "Take one hour to
yourself alone of every day. Buy it, if you must ; but take it.
Occupy it in some interest wholly aside from household or
family care. Bend the bow back which will otherwise be
spoiled by being strained too hard." I have so often been
thanked by those who have tried this rule, that I have been
encouraged to offer it again and again. I have seen so much
misery in homes where a conscientious woman would not
adopt it, that I am compelled to impress it with the more
urgency. Mr. Webster's statement is, that you can do
more in eight hours than in ten. But what he means is,
that if you rightly use the other two, the eight hours are

worth more than the ten would have been unbroken. And
Mr. Webster was a master in this matter of the relationship
between a man's vocation and his avocation.

6. And now I come to a direction vastly more important
than any or all these matters of detail. The mind is beneath your own control, if you will choose to assert that control early. It shall not think of mean things or bad things,
unless you permit it. Not at once, indeed, but yet by slow
training, that control is possible. Yes, and the first direction
is this, of the sensible though enthusiastic Paul, that a man
shall not think of himself,— and he adds, with a certain
humor which never long leaves him indeed, "more highly
than he ought to think"; a condition which, to most of us,
leaves the range of thinking, which is permitted, on a plane
sufficiently if not ludicrously low.

In another statement of St. Paul's, which we cannot consider too often, he says of the Saviour himself: "He made
himself of no reputation." The two phrases together are
the sternest rebuke of this self-conscious thought of one's
self which uses man's noblest power for what is man's
meanest business. Warning enough, or rebuke enough, if
warning and rebuke would save us! And when these do
not save a man,— when he yields to the temptation and uses
his reason only about himself — uses his memory to remember his own affairs only—uses his imagination only to build
his own air-castles — his skill in the mathematics only to compute his own fortune,— then the punishment in store for him
is the punishment most terrible. For the time is before him
when he shall not be able to turn his thought away from the
central figure. He shall go to the theatre to see the marvels of the drama ; but the scene shall pass before his eyes,
he noticing nothing, because he sees nothing but himself ;
he sits acting over some mortifying failure. Or, he shall buy
the last romance and take it home and read ; but there is no
story for him — no lover and no mistress — no plot and no
denouement. He cannot separate himself from these steadily recurring memories, to which he has taught the fibres of
his brain to recur. Or, he shall travel ; but alas ! he takes
his familiar with him, and with mockery, like that of Mephis-·
topheles, in every Alpine valley, in every picture-gallery,
and at every pageant, here the old chatter begins again about
" me " and " mine " and " I " and " myself," which it would
be such mercy to leave at home. Poor wretch, he cannot
leave it at home ! He thought when he was a boy that these

simple words, "He made himself of no reputation," had no meaning for him. He would make himself a name to be trumpeted. He thought, when he read in St. Paul "that no man was to think of himself," that this was an Oriental exaggeration, or it was for eighteen centuries ago; or, briefly, that he knew better than St. Paul. He thought so; but he learned that the punishment for that conceitedness is to be cursed with one's own company, one's own thoughts, one's own memories.

Of which disease, the remedy also is offered by the same physician: "Let a man think soberly," he says; and in another place: "Whatsoever things are pure, whatsoever things are true, whatsoever things are honest, whatsoever things are lovely, whatsoever things are of good report, if there be any virtue or if there be any praise, think on these things." Now this instruction is practical, not meant for rhetoric or poetry, but as a direction for an intelligent man to pursue in the conduct of life. You can keep impure thoughts out of your mind by thinking of that which is pure. You can keep yourself out of your mind by thinking of other people. And, to train the mind in generous and large thought, so that it may not fall back to mean thought and small, is the most important duty you have in this part of life, which has to do with making ready your weapons.

Perhaps it was easier for Paul to press the eternal motive for such exercise than it is for us. Certainly it was easier for these men of Philippi, these freedmen of Rome, to understand it. With just a handful of them, Paul was attacking the gigantic system of terror and crime which upheld a Nero,—which made all men brutes and all women slaves. With fifty men and women in Rome, against five million, he coolly undertook to bring in that higher order, which he called the "Kingdom of God." Not Leonidas at Thermopylæ had such odds against him. Yet Paul meant to succeed; they meant to succeed. And he says to them, that, if they are to succeed, they must be armed and equipped, girt and trained in every point; to fulfil a thousand duties, to bear a thousand perils. "Know ye not that God's temple is holy, which temple ye are?" That is what he says of their bodies. "One of us, one of you, stain this temple by some beastly impurity!—Never!" And they understood and accepted that responsibility. It was not for some crown of their own, simply, that they put under foot this temptation or that. It was for the strength and the victory of the whole company. That appeal is the appeal to us. For yourself, you might choose to take this cursed liquor to your hand and lip till it became your master. For yourself, you might choose to lie on a sofa and read those dirty novels, till you had no will of your own. But you do not live for yourself: nor for yourself will you die. Your death of shame is so much loss from the fighting force; is so much discouragement to your father, your mother, your brother, your sister. Your life of negligence, as you sit, not even dreaming, looking out from a hotel parlor on the busy street, is a life stolen from the great army of the workers who work with God. And your life, worthless when it is tested, your work which breaks to flinders when it is tried, because you would not temper the tool with which you worked, is only so much hindrance to the great army of the sons of God. You can eat the rations,— yes ! There must be a cot in the hospital for you,— oh yes ! But you cannot take your turn on picket. And when the moment of battle comes, you can neither ride, nor take aim, nor so much as walk where you are bidden.

That is not the shame of the living children of a living God. " My father worketh, and I work." That is their motto. To claim it fairly, they keep under their bodies and put them in subjection ; and for their minds, they think on what is pure, honest, true, lovely, and of good report. They think not of themselves more highly than they ought to think. " Every thought is brought into captivity."

From May to November.

A second series of sermons preached by Mr. Hale in the South Congregational Church will be published weekly. After the 6th of September, each sermon will usually be published the Saturday after it is preached.

The sermons already published are—

> THE LIFE IN COMMON,
>
> BODY, MIND, AND SOUL,
>
> BODILY TRAINING,
>
> MENTAL DISCIPLINE.

These sermons are published by GEO. H. ELLIS, 101 Milk Street. Price, 10 cents each, or $1.00 for the series of fifteen.

c V.j

CANDOR IN THE PULPIT.

A SERMON

PREACHED AT THE SOUTH CONGREGATIONAL CHURCH,

BOSTON,

SEPTEMBER 7, 1879,

BY

EDWARD E. HALE.

BOSTON:

GEO. H. ELLIS, PRINTER, 101 MILK STREET.

1879.

CANDOR IN THE PULPIT.

" The truth shall make you free."— JOHN viii., 32.

It is one of the greater benefits derived from a journey or a visit, that we are so glad, when it is ended, to return home. There is the same benefit in the closing of the church for a few weeks: we come back with all the memories of past years to quicken our hopes of years to come; and in a thousand associations with other years, there comes in a special pleasure for this first day at home. I know very well that some of you are strangers here, and do not feel this at all; and I cannot ask that those who are not strangers should feel it as I do, for my whole life and my whole duty centres here, and yours does not. But I may believe that for almost all of us, absence for a few weeks makes the house of our worship all the more homelike and glad.

I will try not to run counter to this line of pleasant feeling in saying something to-day which may seem a little personal, about what you may expect of me, and what you have a right to expect of me, in the services which bring us together here. But I do not mean to speak in the least of myself personally, excepting in one point, and you will see why I do so there. I do want to speak of my special profession, of this business of preaching, because just now there has been more or less public discussion about its responsibilities, and I have not seen that we have had a fair representation yet in that discussion,— we ministers, whose duty it is to preach as well as we can, and from these pulpits to announce the best we know. It seems to me but reasonable — before I begin on another series of fifty sermons, which I want you to come to hear — for me to say, squarely, how much I want to do in such preaching, and to acknowledge, with equal frankness, what are the limitations on me in the nature of things ; that is, to say what I do not expect to do. This I am going to try to say, because it seems to me that in some recent public discussions both our responsibilities and our limitations have been unfairly stated.

Some years since, a New York politician of repute was discussing our system of public affairs with a friend of mine, and among other things they spoke of the place and power of the pulpit. The New Yorker said boldly that the ministers must not be permitted to keep up their talk about higher law, nor in any way to express opinions on matters which might come into a political canvass. My friend, who was used to the New England habits, said if he went to church at all he liked to have a man say what he thought was true, whether he agreed with it himself or not.

"I do not know that," said the other. And this remark I wish to comment on particularly: "These preachers," he said, "make us assent quietly to a great many things which no man of sense believes; and, in return, we have a right to tell them to be quiet with regard to certain matters which we understand better than they can."

There was the frank statement of a man used to compromise and convenience in public affairs, used to what is familiarly called log-rolling. "If I stand by you, you must stand by me." That is its demand. I am afraid that, in all its brutal frankness, his remark expresses only too well an underlying suspicion which exists in many minds, that the clergy or the pulpit have certain secrets which they do not disclose, certain reticences which they are obliged to keep, and that they pretend to believe certain things in which they have no confidence. This man had some reason for saying that the clergy to whom he was accustomed asked him to assent quietly to certain things which no man of sense believed. To take, for the moment, certain extreme cases,— and I will speak by-and-by of cases which are not extreme, — there is certainly not one man of sense in a hundred who believes that at the call of Joshua the sun and moon literally stood still for hours over Gibeon and Ajalon. Yet I hazard nothing in saying that the preachers who controlled the religion of Central New York, where that man lived, would not in ten years' time permit a suspicion to be expressed in their pulpits that the statement in the book of Joshua is not literally true. When people go to church in such a region and listen to these preachers, they are conscious all the time of such buried embers, which must be trodden over very gently. ᵔy sit and listen to sermons which they do not really assent

to, certain that behind there is a great deal which they do
not assent to,— which must not be spoken about by anybody.
The absolute and eternal damnation of ninety-nine hun-
dredths of the human race is such a hidden coal of fire.
This man of whom I speak probably did ' not believe it ;
probably none of the men of intelligence around him believed
it ; probably the minister whom he heard on Sunday did not
believe it. But, because the doctrine is all wrought in with
the whole system of the church establishment to which they
belonged, and because they all believed that it was best to
maintain some system of united worship and of church life,
they dreaded to pull out this particular offending tenet, and
all tacitly agreed to let it pass with as little allusion to it as
might be possible.

So large is the mass of these hidden unbeliefs, that it has
lately been squarely charged on the clergy, in quarters which
give great weight to such a charge, that they are consciously
keeping back what they know; and this is said by way of
accounting for the indifference with which people hear them.
It is said that perhaps if they suppress so much which is true,
they may express what is false ; or, if the case be not quite
so bad as this, it is said that people have not absolute
confidence in the sincerity of the pulpit. It is said that
people think we are keeping up a form, and that what we say
is of no great account, because what we do not say — what
we are afraid to say — is a mass of hidden truth important
and formidable.

I heard a minister of another communion from ours express it in this way : —

" I think," said he, " that if Tyndall or Huxley lectured
in the Music Hall on one of our subjects,— say on education, or on the relief of the poor, which every one would
say were our subjects,— I think that the audience of three
thousand people there would believe that Tyndall or Huxley
were telling the very best he knew, and telling it precisely
as well as he could. I think the audience would believe
in his sincerity. But if one of us ministers were to speak
in the Music Hall on one of their subjects,— on evolution,
or the law of natural selection, or the creation of the
world,— I do not think that all that audience would trust us
in the same way. 1 think many persons would doubt our
sincerity, because we are clergymen. For we are constantly
stating as truths so many things which we cannot prove, that

I think many persons have lost their confidence in our sincerity, and consider us as people who, in the interests of a cause, overstate, understate, or are in some other way indifferent to accuracy."

Now, when I heard this estimate, passed by an experienced minister on his own profession, I felt as if my hair grew gray as he spoke. I could hardly believe my ears. If I thought my hearers supposed me to be such a rhetorician as he described, so indifferent to accuracy, so insincere, I would never stand in any pulpit again. What comfort is there in speaking, what pleasure, what use, if, while you speak, you know that people do not believe half you say? You are worse off than an actor is ; for he, for the moment, carries his hearer with him, and though the people do not believe he is Shylock or Hamlet, they do believe the sentiment which he utters from Shylock's mouth or Hamlet's. It is about six months since I heard this confession made by a preacher. I do not know that any statement regarding my profession has ever affected me so sadly. At once I made it subject of thought and inquiry. I wanted to know whether it fairly describes the estimate which men have of us, which people in general have about preachers, or which you have about me.

Well, I am not fully prepared to answer all of those questions to-day. But I am sorry to say that I fear that this gentleman's suspicions are partly true. I think the opinion of the New York politician whom I cited goes a good way among men of the pews,— men of the world, as perhaps they would call themselves. I must speak of separate cases, though I do not want to be invidious. Wherever a church chooses to anchor itself to an old creed, it is necessarily in great danger. Here are our friends of the American Episcopal Church. All their tendencies are to breadth. They do not want to be narrow. If they have any central wish, it is to be the national church, embracing all the Christians of the land. But, unhappily for them, they have anchored themselves to three or four creeds which are by no means consistent with each other. There is the Apostles' Creed which says one thing, and the Nicene Creed which says more things, and their brethren in England add the Athanasian Creed which says more ; and some of them think that it would be best for them to believe all that the English Church believes. Then there are the Thirty-nine Articles of religion, which say many more things. In practice, any man may join the Episcopal Church and receive its sacraments, who, in any fashion, believes the Apostles' Creed. They would receive me, not as a preacher but as a layman. without any objection. But, all the same, the Prayer-book contains the Nicene Creed and the Thirty-nine Articles,—or, if it be an English Prayer-book, the Athanasian Creed beside. And there is no doubt that the impression is,— and the fair impression, too,— that these creeds, or certainly the first three I named, contain the doctrine of the Episcopal Church as the clergy receive it. There are some dioceses where the bishop would not ordain a minister unless he believed from his heart the Apostles' Creed, the Nicene Creed, and the Thirty-nine Articles.

Now, in every Episcopal Church this Prayer-book is in every pew. The thoughtful layman opens on the Thirty-nine Articles. He reads, for instance, that Christ, after rising from the dead, took with him into heaven " his flesh, bones, and all things pertaining to the perfection of man's nature, and there sitteth until he return to judge all men the last day."

He does not believe this ; he knows he does not believe it. He does not believe that the flesh, bones, and body which Jesus Christ wore in Galilee are in any place outside this world. But he thinks the man in a surplice, in the pulpit opposite, has said he does believe it. What follows is, that he thinks the minister careless and inaccurate in his expression of his opinions ; or, he considers him a hypocrite, professing for comfort's sake an opinion that he does not entertain at all. It has been said by a witty man that there is not one man of sense in the nineteenth century who really believes one of the Thirty-nine Articles. It is certain that if, by good luck, they could be blotted out of being to-night, if a synod of the Episcopal Church met to-morrow to state articles of belief, they would not repeat one of those articles in the form in which it stands. It is certain that they are bound into the Prayer-book as a bit of history, and because it is hard to get them out. But, all the same, it is certain that the mass of men — the rank and file who know anything about them — believe that the clergy of that church have expressed a belief in them. This is not quite true. What is true is, that the clergy of that church have not expressed their disbelief in them. While they do not, while they let such a bit of old times and forgotten opinion lie, they undoubtedly get the reputation among practical people of pretending to believe something they do not believe. They suffer, therefore, from that reputation of insincerity of which I am inquiring.

Now I do not select the Episcopal Church as more in danger than other churches with written creeds. I select it because it is, on the whole, the broadest of all churches which are so unfortunate. The suspicion which falls on their clergy falls on the Roman Catholic priest when he says the wafer is God. The layman does not believe it, and he is apt to think that in his heart the priest does not believe it. When the layman in one of our Orthodox Congregational churches hears the old-fashioned creed of his church read, knowing that he would never have chosen that language to express his own convictions,— wondering that the minister believes what he does not believe,— he is in danger of suspecting the minister's sincerity. Even our friends the Methodists,— who are very broad, who want to be broad,— in New England, are not afraid of the name latitudinarian,— are trammelled by the same tangle. Twenty years ago I said to one of the wisest and best of them, that they also had one creed for the pulpit and another for the pews. He said it was not so. He said I could be received to their ordination without assent to the articles, if I would only say I loved Christ,— as I gladly could say, in the sense he meant. But he said I should have to say that I did not mean to break up the organization. And I could not make him see the hollowness of a system which puts in print certain articles of religion, supposing it well to keep them before the world, when at heart the men who are to carry out that system do not believe those articles at the bottom of their souls.

That I do not state the danger with any unfairness, let me read you words from an authority every one will own to be competent. I could not make the statement with more severity. Here is what Mr. Phillips Brooks said in a recent address, which has been printed in the *Princeton Review.* He is speaking at a school of theology : —

"And first of all, as the most needed," he says, " and I am tempted to say as the most rare, of the qualities that such a man must have, I cannot hesitate to speak of candor. The scepticism which I have been trying to describe evidently must be a very pervading thing. It evidently cannot be shut up in any pervading class or classes. Life plays upon faith everywhere. Ideas change and develop in all

sorts and conditions of men. And the occupants of pulpits,
the preachers, have their doubts and disbeliefs as well as
others. The first step, I believe, towards a clear relationship between the preacher and the people ought to be a perfectly frank understanding of this fact. There ought to be
not the least concealment or disguise about it. Men ought
never to have the slightest reason to suppose that the
preacher is asking them to believe what he does not believe
himself, or warning them that it is dangerous to doubt what
to his own mind seems very questionable. But how is it
now? A large acquaintance with clerical life has led me to
think that almost any company of clergymen, gathering together and talking freely to each other, will express opinions
which would greatly surprise and at the same time greatly
relieve the congregations who ordinarily listen to those
ministers. Now just see what that means. It means that
in these days when faith is hard we are deliberately making
it harder, and are making ourselves liable to the Master's
terrible rebuke of the Scribes and Pharisees of old : 'They
bind heavy burdens, and grievous to be borne, and lay them
on men's shoulders, but they themselves will not move them
with one of their fingers.' Is not this true? How many
men in the ministry to-day believe in the doctrine of verbal
inspiration which our fathers held, and how many of us have
frankly told the people that we do not believe it, and so
lifted off their Bible's page the heavy cloud of difficulties
and inconsistencies which that doctrine laid there?"
   ... "Not much more than a year ago, I heard one of
our most venerable preachers deliberately tell a congregation that no man was a Christian who did not believe that
this world was made in six literal days. He had a perfect
right to say so if he thought so, as no doubt he did. But
for those of us whom any such test of Christianity would
totally exclude from any claim to Christian character, to let
such statements pass without most clear and earnest disa-
vowals is certainly a grievous wrong to faith, and makes the
scepticism against which it tries to guard.
   "There must be no lines of orthodoxy inside the lines of
truth. Men find that you are playing with them, and will
not believe you even when you come in earnest. I know
what may be said in answer. I know the old talk about
holding the outworks as long as we can, and then retreating
to the citadel ; and perhaps there has hardly been a more
mischievous metaphor than this. It is the mere illustration

of a metaphor. The minister who tries to make people believe that which he questions, in order to keep them from questioning that which he believes, knows very little about the certain workings of the human heart, and has no real faith in truth itself."

Now, at the beginning of another year's preaching, I cite these statements from different people, and I point out these dangers of the creed-bound churches, simply because I want to say, that these gentlemen must speak for their own churches and communions, and not for those of us who are not fettered by unchanging creeds. When it is said that a minister is not candid, let us know what church says that, and of what ministers it is said. This statement of Mr. Brooks has been widely cited. The president of the university cited it,—speaking immediately after Mr. Brooks, and when I was to follow him immediately. He cited it to show why young men would not come into the pulpit,—because they thought the pulpit was insincere. And certainly, if the pulpit is going to accept the charge of want of candor or of insincerity, the sooner honest men learn it, and the more sternly honest men keep out of it, the better for them and for the world.

Now you have seen how squarely Mr. Brooks protests against any such want of candor. But Mr. Brooks feels the danger, and confesses it, of lines of orthodoxy inside lines of truth.

Our position in the liberal pulpit is more fortunate. With our eyes open, knowing the difficulties of our position, we and our fathers in these liberal churches determined not to have any lines of orthodoxy. We have our views as to truth, but, with our eyes open, we determined that every man must state his own creed, and that no one must be called on to accept any he had not stated. In this course, there are great inconveniences. The world is not yet used to it, and handles us very unfairly. If a man who calls himself a Unitarian in Nebraska says he ought to have five wives at a time, there are plenty of people to say that the Unitarians believe everybody ought to have five wives. Every one of us is constantly taken to task for absurdities committed in the Unitarian name. But as I said, with our eyes open to the inconveniences,—if you please, to the disadvantages,—of our position, we assumed that position. We state no creed,—

not about God, Christ, Bible, Heaven, or Hell; not about
the things people most agree upon : because we know the
danger of having " lines of orthodoxy inside the lines of
truth." Let every man state his own.

Taking these disadvantages, we are entitled, any fair man
would say, to the advantages of this position. It is not fair
to hold any Unitarian preacher responsible for the absurdities, or the lack of faith, or the lack of candor, of the communions which have chosen to write down their beliefs, and
are trying to cling to those lines, however strongly the tide of
opinion and of life may sweep them away. Our skirts are
clear. This pulpit never said that this world was made in
six literal days. This pulpit never said that the sun stood
still upon Gibeon, nor the moon in the valley of Ajalon.
This pulpit never said we must hold the outworks of belief
as long as we can, before we retreat to the citadel. Not in
my day, nor in my predecessor's day, nor in his venerable
predecessor's, was any such homage paid here, either to
decorum or to tradition. The people who founded this
church wrenched the ties which bound them to such decorous
observances, though it cost them tears of blood. Those who
followed them have taken frankly all the inconveniences, all
the opprobriums, of freedom. And they are entitled, in
return, at least to the credit of sincerity and candor.

I have myself supposed that the danger of our pulpit was
on the other side. There is an affectation of candor, as
there may be an affectation of justice and an affectation of
mercy. It is as absurd as any affectation. I have thought
the Unitarian pulpit was in danger of that affectation. I
have heard a Unitarian preacher say in prayer, " We bring
thee our best thoughts of to-day, and our best hopes and
faith. If to-morrow we reject them, we will be first to disown them before thy throne." I think this is carrying sincerity into affectation. I think no man speaks so to the
friend whom he trusts, or the woman whom he loves. No
man feels bound by candor or sincerity to say, " I am very
fond of you to-day, and if to-morrow I see anybody I like
better, I will be first to tell you so." It is of this affectation
of sincerity that I have thought we were in more danger than
of the lack of candor.

I have thought, again, that we were in danger of passing
into absurd rashness in our courage or independence. One
of our preachers took occasion to say that we ought to place
in the pulpit the Bhagavat-Gita, the collection of the wis-

dom of India, instead of this antiquated Hebrew Bible. Freeman Clarke replied, "Will you have it in Sanscrit or in English?" "Oh, I would read from the English, of course," said the young reformer. "And how will you do that," said his wiser friend, "seeing it has never been translated?" A few passages, versions made through the French, were, in fact, all that were at that time in the English tongue. And the brave reformer, too ignorant to know that the book did not exist in English, was yet bold enough to urge that it should be used as a substitute for the Bible. That sort of audacity, sublime in its intent, preposterous in the detail, is one of the dangers that we have brought on ourselves by assuming the liberal position. If we accept the dangers of such audacity, we ought to be free from the disgraces of supposed concealment or want of candor.

I certainly hope that friends of mine of twenty years' standing here, know that, for one, I have nothing to conceal in the pulpit. What I know I will tell ; what I believe I will say. I will not often trouble you by telling what I do not know,— that would take long indeed. And I will grant, as you have heard me say a thousand times, that I know no prayer so sublime, or which so well expresses our position here before God, as the prayer of the poor man in Galilee: "Lord, I believe ; help thou mine unbelief." But I do not choose to leave the imputation of want of candor or insincerity on the issue of any personal feeling you may have about me. I am anxious to say, as publicly as I can, in reference to what Mr. Brooks has said, that I also have a large acquaintance with clerical life. I have frequent opportunities of hearing ministers in private communion,— the most private. As such communion has been alluded to, I am bound to bear testimony to the simple piety, the dependence upon God, of the clergymen whom I have known most prominent in affairs and best known before the world. I think that congregations, and the larger world which does not affect church-going, would be surprised and would be comforted, if, with propriety, they could hear, see, and feel the simplicity and tenderness of the religious faith of the men whom the public regard as the intellectual or logical or ecclesiastical leaders of the religious institutions of the country. And as for secrets in theology not made known to the world, I am bound to say that so far as we are concerned there are no such hidden mysteries. There are wide differences of opinion among our clergy, undoubtedly. But a free pulpit gives every man a chance, and, as I have said, offers a temptation for a complete exposure of them. Even if a man *were* a coward, he has no motive in our time for concealment.

Two years ago, for instance, at the movement of some of our most radical and most conservative men, an arrangement was made for an Institute, on the plan of the Social Science meetings, or those of the Scientific Association. It was a meeting of ministers, without lay delegates, at Springfield ; arranged that men might tell the last thing they had learned in American freethinking, in German criticism, in Eastern research. I know it was proposed that the meetings should be private ; but so soon as it was found that the Springfield people wanted to listen, the doors were thrown open. But the same papers were read then which were prepared for the clergy only. The lowest depth of research was sounded, and the soundings were exposed to anybody who wanted to look on. The second session of this Institute, as it is called, will be held next month in Providence.

Or let me take an illustration from the other side. I have the honor to belong to a philosophical club of which one-quarter of the members are clergymen. The others are artists, authors, merchants, or manufacturers. The subjects discussed range through the whole circle of speculation, from the theory of laws of prohibition round to the origin of the idea of beauty. I am bound to say that, so far as I can see, the seven or eight clergymen in that club are, on the whole, the audacious speculators. They have, on the whole, read the most, and, on the whole, they are the least anxious about consequences. They believe that the truth will take care of itself, and, on the whole, are least distressed about guards and barriers for its preservation.

This is to be said in conclusion, however, and I wish I could so say it that it could be remembered : —

People judge the pulpit, judge the minister, by what he says on one occasion,— or what they think he says. That is very unfair. A sermon is a mere bit in a great mosaic. It has a beginning, middle, and end, but it belongs to a long series of instructions,— a series which covers many years. It is very unfair to expect a man to put into one sermon all he knows, all he believes, all he does not know, and all he does not believe. I have probably said in this pulpit five hundred times in twenty-two years, that I suppose what we call the Gospels are broken fragments of memoirs collected at different times, between the thirtieth and sixtieth years after the Saviour's death ; that it is a great pity there are not more ; and that it is very hard to reconstruct the history from such fragments. It is very hard to be expected, by an occasional church-goer, to say that, every Sunday before I read from the gospel,—hard not only on me, but on those who come to church more frequently than he. And here is only one instance in a thousand, where we have a right to claim, that what we say and what we do not say in any sermon shall be judged not by that sermon only, but with fair reference to what we have said before.

Judge us, dear friends, as you would be judged. I do not speak of myself only, but of all who try to tell God's truth in the pulpit. "Who is sufficient for these things?" Paul asks, eagerly. Of course nobody is sufficient for them. Nobody but a fool ever thought he was sufficient. But we are sufficient to do the work in part. We can tell the best we know. We can report the message we have heard. We can study a little, and tell you what we have learned. We can talk with the saints on earth, and do our best to interpret what they tell us. Trust us so far. And we,— we will promise to tell no lies. Whatever the trumpet sounds,— faint if you please, unmusical if you please,— it shall not be uncertain.

The truth shall make us free, and freedom will compel the truth. We may all rest on these certainties: God is true and we are his children. We really know the tone of his voice. We know when a true child of his tells what he believes. This divine instinct is our birthright because we are God's children. No rhetoric will deceive us ; no ingenious logic will do more than confuse us : no authority will alarm us. Listen as the true children of a true God, speak as the true children of a true God, and he the Spirit of Truth will come, and into all truth he will guide you!

From Thanksgiving to Fast.

FIFTEEN SERMONS

BY

EDWARD E. HALE.

THE GREAT HARVEST YEAR,
LOOKING BACK,
RITUAL,
PRAYER,
RESPECTABILITY,
YOURSELVES,
WHAT IT IS TO BE CATHOLIC,
THE JOY OF LIFE,
THE ASSOCIATED CHARITIES,
THE REVISION OF THE BIBLE,
THE BIBLE,
LENT,
NEW LIFE,
BLASPHEMY AGAINST THE HOLY GHOST,
THE FUTURE OF NEW ENGLAND.

Price in paper covers, $1.00; in cloth binding, $1.25.

A second series (of fifteen) of Mr. Hale's sermons is now being issued, of which there have already been printed

THE LIFE IN COMMON,
BODY, MIND, AND SOUL,
BODILY TRAINING,
MENTAL DISCIPLINE,
CANDOR IN THE PULPIT.

Price, 10 cents per copy, or $1.00 for the series. Published by GEO. H. ELLIS, 101 Milk Street, Boston.

SPIRITUAL EXERCISES.

A SERMON

PREACHED AT THE SOUTH CONGREGATIONAL CHURCH,

BOSTON,

JUNE 22, 1879,

BY

EDWARD E. HALE.

BOSTON:

GEO. H. ELLIS, PRINTER, 101 MILK STREET.

1879.

SPIRITUAL EXERCISES.

In Him we live, and move, and have our being.— ACTS xviii., 28.

A thoughtful critic of the recent English novels says that the good people in them — the people who have to meet trials and do right — make no reference to religion as the source of this power. The trials and temptations of these modern novels are tremendous. A certain sombre and even lurid or stormy character sweeps over life as they describe it ; and these trials and temptations are bravely borne. There would be no novel, there would be neither hero nor heroine, were there not some one who, on the whole, resists evil and overcomes evil with good. All the interest of any tale, from the very simplest, comes from such control and such victory ; but it is said that the victor does not now claim to triumph in the name of the Father or of the Son or of the Holy Spirit.

In Dr. Watts' day it was different : —

> " I asked them whence their victory came :
> With one united breath
> They owed their conquest to the Lamb,
> Their triumph to his death."

And the experienced novel-reader will remember that the school of English fiction goes through a series of regular stages in this business. Defoe's stories, Robinson Crusoe, Col. Jack, and the rest, contain passages of distinct religious instruction and suggestion which might be preached for sermons, and would make very good sermons. But in Fielding's and Smollett's stories, all the more in Mrs. Behn's, distinct religious instruction or religious teachers would seem out of place, as much as in a circus performance to-day. The story may not be wrong, but you are glad there is no pretext at distinctly religious motive. Scott is always decorous with regard to religion. But his hermit or field preacher or bishop play their parts in the story rather by the strength of their right arms, or, at best, the quickness of their wits, than by moral forces or the higher spiritual power. Miss Austen and Miss Edgeworth seldom allude to prayer,

Bible, Heaven, or God. The machinery of their books goes on with almost as little religious allusion as a text-book of arithmetic. Then there came in a curious period when the moral miracles of novels were wrought by good doctors. When everything was at a dead lock, a doctor came in who was upright and pure and wise, and had his wisdom from above, also. He taught the ignorant, and comforted the sad, and waked the dormant, and shrived the dying and led them to the fountain of life indeed. And then came in the "religious novel," so-called, which has, I hope, had its day. To the reaction from it, perhaps, we may ascribe the non-religion of our present school. It is non-religion, not irreligion. When the entanglement was sufficient, a distinct teacher of religion appeared, generally a clergyman, ordained in the way the novelist thought right,— in one way in Miss Yonge's stories or Miss Sewell's, in others in Mrs. Charles's, in yet others in Mrs. Stowe's and Miss Warner's. Perhaps it was not a clergyman. Perhaps it was a little girl who had been well instructed. This person applied the remedy, taught the lesson, reformed the sinner, shrived the repentant, and all was well. That system, rather overdone, has perhaps done its work for a generation; and now we have stories, as I said, where the word religion does not appear, and, on the other hand, reference to religious obligation is distinctly disavowed.

All the same, you will observe that Mr. Hardy's stories or Mr. Black's, which are those particularly referred to by the critic I cited, have people who tell the truth, do right, keep their bodies in subjection, and suffer terribly for good and truth and duty. So is it in George's Eliot's novels, of which the same general remark may often be made. This must be. All interest would die out of a mere chaffy collection,— I might say of anecdotes, how John did this and Jane did that, — if they were not threaded upon a struggle and a victory. And this victory has to imply a victory of good over evil, of right over wrong, or the impartial human soul will not long accept the books. Fiction seems to have no charm in the long run, unless it present the eternal truth that the soul of man is greater than his senses and his sense,— than his body and his intellectual machinery.

It is precisely this training of the child of God himself, that he may rule mind and body, which I want to speak of to-day, in a set of practical recipes, if you please, just as I spoke to the young people of the training of body and the training of mind. Will, character, force, command, success, — these do not belong to body nor to mind. They sway body and mind. How are you going to obtain them, so that body and mind shall not upset the whole concern, and set it drifting on the sea of life, like a capsized ship whose top-hamper is all helplessly dragging in the sea, instead of giving the direction and movement to the whole? In your daily training, what are to be the exercises of the soul, the mind's master and the body's? Granted that they are different from the spiritual exercises of Thomas à Becket, or from those of Oliver Cromwell, or from those of Samuel Adams. Still there must be spiritual exercises. And there must be such exercises every day. Grant that a man is not to tell a string of beads every day. Grant that he is not to read a stinted fraction of the Breviary. Grant that he is not to go to morning and evening chapel as if he were in a college. Grant that he is not to read two chapters of the Bible on week-days and five on Sundays, so as to finish it in a year. Still, nothing grows but by exercise. And if manhood is to grow or womanhood is to grow, the soul must be exercised. And, again, just as we have seen in mental training and in physical, this exercise cannot be crowded on one day in the week, nor can it be crowded on one week or one month·in a year. It is an exercise which must recur every day in life, as steadily as the rising of the sun and the passage of morning into noon, and of noon into evening, and evening into night.

I. Any point in space may be fixed by reference to three coördinates, or lines traced in three different directions. If one be upward, one forward and backward, and a third at a definite angle from these two in another plane, you have, of course, all the latitudes and longitudes you want, so to speak, to define the place of any body. That familiar enough fact is a good illustration of the way in which Paul's three great words give the points of reference and measurement for all life, and so the ways of directing it. "Upward, forward, or around," all life, and all training for life, must come into categories which belong to these three central directions. And a man's spiritual exercises come under the head of Faith, in which he looks above himself; of Hope, in which he looks forward from this moment; and of Love, in which he looks all around, outside of his own existence and career.

I am to give my practical prescriptions for these three sets of daily exercises. And we will take them in the reverse order.

II. Do not let us be too grand. Let us plant our seed at first in a flower-pot, under our own eyes. When it has grown, we can transplant into the flower-garden, the nursery, or the orchard. Let us begin at home. I remember having to advise a man who had fallen into a sad because a morose life, and had put himself under my counsel; and I said: "Suppose you begin by passing the butter at table." He needed to be on the outlook, consciously, for little occasions to serve those around him. Life at a restaurant, and hotel-life in foreign countries, perhaps, where you distrust those who do not speak your language, might make you lonesome and self-caring. Take care in the least exercises that you care for others. "I do not like the man," said a sound observer to me; "I saw he let his wife pick up her own handkerchief." This critic was right in that quick judgment. "I judge him by the way he treats his dog." That is a wise criticism. And if it is wise in criticism, it is wise in life. Train yourself to unselfishness in what the world pleases to call little things.

I remember one of the saints — whom God called up higher long ago — as you saw her when you entered a room where she was sitting. Invariably she laid by her book or put down her needle for the moment, till she saw whether she could help you who came in. She was not obtrusive: simply she was ready. If you wanted her advice, her information, her society, there it was. If not, in a moment she returned to her affairs. Now I do not say in that particular method, but in that spirit, is the principle of the whole thing. That saint knew that she did not live for herself alone. So do you; so do all of us. But she had contrived this daily exercise,— ten thousand times better than telling beads or reading breviaries,— by which to make a habit and practice of what she knew. The power which is gained in such self-control is power which tells in the great martyr-doms and the infinite victories.

The truth is, indeed, that we are ourselves in danger from our New England habit of keeping secret what we feel. The New Englander's reticency seems to be a cross between the English shyness and the Indian's stoicism. There is plenty of feeling, but the feeling does not show itself. Now, this is bad for all parties. It is bad for you who keep the secret of

your love, and it is bad for those you love, who have a right
to know it. Remember that awful story of John Foster.
He idolized his son, but he kept his love so secret from the
young man that he never knew it till within an hour of his
death. Then, from his father's agony, the young man de-
tected this secret of a life, and tried to reassure his father by
saying, "I die happy, for I know now what I have never
dreamed of,—how well you love me." Now that reticence,
that lack of demonstration, as people call it, was as bad for
John Foster as it was for his boy. Mercy blesses him who
gives, as well as him who takes. And this is true of every
effort of the man outside a selfish life. There is, then, one
of the infinite lessons involved in that counsel of a woman
of large experience to a youngster in the midst of his first
certainty of successful love. "Never give up the romance of
this beginning." That is good advice to all young men and
all young women. Though you grow to be as old as John
Anderson, you are not too old for the moss rose-buds, the
wave of the handkerchief, the kiss of the hand, and the welcome at the open door which were so charming at seventeen.
And to this general principle belongs the general remark,
that home and home life must never become commonplace.
The little surprises, the remembrance of the birthday, the
unexpected treat, the pleasure earned for one by the sacrifice
of another,— all these belong under our head of spiritual exercises. Nor is there any scene of our life which so demands
such exercise as this familiar scene of home, which has to
be reset every day.

But I am not willing to leave such exercises simply in the
routine of home life. It is quite possible, though not perhaps usual, for people to be kindly, and even tender, in their
home relations, while the family, as a family, is hard and
cold in its relations to the outside world. "We" and "our
house" have, in such cases, become a sort of House of
Lords, an aristocracy of a higher grade; and outside "our
family" nobody must expect to be privileged by our special
attention. This danger is so palpable that every prudent
person will be on the lookout for it. Ask yourself, not too
often, but sometimes, whether you have at least one distinct
relation which calls you every day outside your own house in
unselfish attention to some other human being. It is your
regular visit to your paralytic neighbor; it is your work of
the sewing-school or the flower mission; it is your walk home
from the store with John, who is apt to be moody if left

alone; it is dropping in at the Christian Union to see if you can be of service there; it is calling at the Brunswick to make certain that those strangers from Texas are made welcome; it is taking your turn on the committees of the South Friendly or the Associated Charities. No difficulty in finding the place, if one have only the pluck to fill it. The rule is certain, that, as a spiritual exercise, every man and woman should have, every day, some unselfish interest involving personal effort outside of home.

It would be easy, of course, to give a thousand illustrations of such exercises of life, which come because ours is a common life; but these are enough. To some such exercise must a person devote part of every day. And it is exercises not unlike these which he needs every day, because his future is infinite, and he wants to live as a person who has an infinite future; he wants to practice now and here in an angel's accomplishments. Because he is to live forever, he chooses to begin to live as one who lives forever.

This is no poor matter of arguing about immortality, of examining the evidences or the analogies. As Mr. Weiss says, admirably, " It is one thing to believe in immortality : it is quite another thing to live as an immortal." Now it is this last thing which we are now talking about. And every young man and young woman must get in the habit, in some of these exercises of every day, of taking up an angel's view of things; that forward look, that wish to conquer, and that certainty of conquest which are in an immortal's nature.

For it is not enough to have these infinite yearnings and faculties. We want to exercise them, to train them, that they also may grow.

Here is the reason why Paul and all the Christian masters put *Hope* so in the fore-front as they do,— sister, indeed, of Love and of Faith. No man in daily life ought to be satisfied with what his life now is. He ought every day to be looking forward to some of the possible improvements. That "man never is but always to be blest," is not a cynical ridicule of man's unrest, as it is sometimes cited : it is a mere commonplace statement of the truth that man, as a child of God, cannot be satisfied with any earthly environment. He always wants more, and he always ought to; for he is God's child, and from God he is always receiving.

Here is the reason why what is called castle-building is often excellent good spiritual exercise. Only take care that you are not yourself the lord and hero of the castle. The danger lies there. But to build up in their detail visions of the future which may be and ought to be, is one of the first steps towards making it certain that that future shall be. To make out the picture of the comfort and happiness of those poor children who are destitute, of the village that is badly governed, of the family that is badly trained, is the beginning of the resolute duty which shall mend all these wrongs. Fear not to do that. Such is a Saviour's direction, for it is your Father's good pleasure to give you the kingdom.

To such study of the possible improvement of the circumstances around a man, a fair share of his daily training ought to be devoted. He has not only the right, but it is his duty, to say, "I am not placed here to live forever at what I do. I am not to be always balancing this ledger, digging out these stumps, copying these invoices, measuring these calicoes, punching these rivet-holes. I am a son, and a favored son, of God Almighty; I am a staff officer of Jesus Christ, and a staff officer whom he loves. By such high commissions am I required — while I do my duty at this humble outpost — to be reconnoitring the open country and making ready for the advance. This is the daily mood, and so the daily exercise, of the man who forgets the things that are behind, and reaches forth unto those that are before.

By the same token, and for like reasons, a man because he is God's child maintains his intimacy with his Father. Mere *creatures* of God may be supposed to keep out of his presence unless they are called. But children come and go as they will. His house is their house. His presence is their home. To cite Mr. Weiss again,— for his spirituality of life makes him a person to be always cited in these considerations,— the child of God listens often to see what his Father has to say to him. I have repeated these words here a thousand times,— none too often, if we have succeeded at all in forming the habit which they demand. To secure solitude, unaffectedly and without observation, once at least in every day, to dismiss other thought and anxiety that one may listen to the will of God, or think out what it is,— this is the centre of a man's spiritual exercise on the side of faith. Nor need I attempt to describe or to put limits to such intimacy,— or, if you please to call it so, such meditation. A friend of mine expressed some surprise that a lady spoke of her Heavenly Father so intimately. "Does that surprise you?" she said; "it is nothing to what I say to Him when we are alone." Such a sense of nearness, of relationship, and of confidence grows in proportion as one uses it and relies upon it. Why, you might be sure of that, from the counter-truth that it declines when you do not use it and do not rely upon it. As for nearness, nothing need be said. That we live and move and have our being in this Infinite Power all around us, which asserts itself in every pulse of life, in every sound, in every perfume and color,— that this is near us, nay, in us, nobody need say or prove. But that we belong to this Power and He to us, that He is conscious of our strivings and we of Him,— this is what Jesus Christ tells us we shall learn if we will try. To try that experiment, to plunge into the ocean of God's life and see if he will not bear us up in a Father's arms,— this is to pray. It is to attempt nothing serious without the thought or word which asks him to help, and make the endeavor his. It is to come to him in every sorrow, talk it over, and recognize him as sympathizing in our failure. It is as well to come to him in every great delight, to thank him for the quickening of our power which has gained success, and to recognize him as sympathizing in our joy.

The older form of religious exercises prescribed fixed hours in a day when men made such acknowledgment of joy or of failure. We do not gain by abandoning them. Men who live together, as men do in college, may well meet together to sing a hymn or repeat a prayer in sympathy. For a family to sing together, or to read a few verses of Scripture, or to join in simple prayer, before the strain and burden of the day begin, is as natural and easy as that they should meet at breakfast, instead of having their meals sent to them at their different rooms. But such exercises by no means cover the whole necessity. The habit of daily exercise of which we are talking is quite independent of ceremonies, even as simple as these. You want to connect the present power of God, I do not say with all your thoughts, but with your real exigencies and your more important undertakings. I knew a man who told me that the coolness of the pillow as he put his head on it at night always spoke to him of the love of God,— gave him the text, "He giveth his beloved sleep," so that it became of course to go to sleep in prayer. Many men would say something like that of the song of morning birds ; so closely does Milton's morning hymn twine in every sound and sight of morning with the God to whom belongs the renewal of life. The "practice of the presence of God" will bring to every man the habit of seeing God in the mist, the cloud, and the curling wave ; of hearing him in every sound ; of resting in his arms when we are tired, and exulting in his strength when we are at work. I am always obliged to any man who, instead of saying "Good-bye" to me, says "God bless you," which means just the same thing. I am glad to have him recognize with me that here are not two of us, but three. And here is the reason why we always ask you to make of every meal a sacrament, by filling the cup or by breaking the bread with such memory of the Saviour's love and the Father's presence as may give to the whole family, to the whole household, the divine and infinite impulse. They eat then indeed of bread from heaven.

These are all simple exercises, indeed : so much the better. A thousand times better than any forms directed by the rubrics of a formulary. So soon, indeed, as a service becomes a mere form, so soon is its value lost. That needs no argument. To see an assembly of students vying in chapel with their director,—which shall gallop fastest along the verses of their alternate psalm, so that the exercise of the day may be finished the sooner,— is a sad enough mockery of all methods of devotion. No ! We do not want to rest on methods, but we do want the reality. And we want the reality every day. Because a day is crowded, we do not want God crowded out of it. Because we have the "joy of eventful living," we do not want to forget the Lord of Life from whom we are born. We are willing to serve Him. We are glad of his help and inspiration. Every day, then, is glad of a new method, if it can find one. And it is well for us if every hour can speak with some new voice, help us with some new hint, lead us by some new inducement, to express our joy that "we live, and move, and have our being in our God." .

The next sermon of this series will be HOME.

From Thanksgiving to Fast.

FIFTEEN SERMONS

BY

EDWARD E. HALE.

THE GREAT HARVEST YEAR,
LOOKING BACK,
RITUAL,
PRAYER,
RESPECTABILITY,
YOURSELVES,
WHAT IT IS TO BE CATHOLIC,
THE JOY OF LIFE,
THE ASSOCIATED CHARITIES,
THE REVISION OF THE BIBLE,
THE BIBLE,
LENT,
NEW LIFE,
BLASPHEMY AGAINST THE HOLY GHOST,
THE FUTURE OF NEW ENGLAND.

Price in paper covers, $1.00; in cloth binding, $1.25.

A second series (of fifteen) of **Mr. Hale's** sermons is now being issued, of which there have already been printed

THE LIFE IN COMMON,
BODY, MIND, AND SOUL,
BODILY TRAINING,
MENTAL DISCIPLINE,
CANDOR IN THE PULPIT,
SPIRITUAL EXERCISES.

Price, 10 cents per copy, or $1.00 for the series. Published by GEO. H. ELLIS, 101 Milk Street, Boston.

HAPPY HOMES.

A SERMON

PREACHED BEFORE THE FIRST RELIGIOUS SOCIETY, ROXBURY,
JULY 20, 1879, AND AT THE CHURCH OF THE MESSIAH,
NEW YORK, AUGUST 24, 1879,

BY

EDWARD E. HALE.

BOSTON:
GEO. H. ELLIS, PRINTER, 101 MILK STREET.
1879.

Press of Geo. H. Ellis, 101 Milk Street.

HAPPY HOMES.

Of a hundred novels tracing the fortunes of young life, ninety-nine end in the happy establishment of a home. Hunted up and down through a thousand dangers, terrified here and terrified there, a young happy husband and his young happy wife struggle out at the end of all traps and all surprises, and turn to smile their sweetest on the reader as they look their last on him, just as they open the door which is to admit them into the untold blessings of a happy home. Thus precisely does the novel,— that great revealer of life in its passions, its intentions, and its successes,— thus precisely does the novel show what is the chief and central work and duty of life,— the creation of a happy home.

To the same effect one of our leading statesmen speaks : "They will tell you," says Mr. Frisbie Hoar in substance, "that the object of government is to place twelve honest men in a jury box." That was, I think Erskine's definition. "They will tell you of this or that detail, like that. But at bottom, the reason men form government, and the object for which government is to be sustained, is that men may live in happy homes."

So is it that when the prodigal son comes to himself after the infatuation of self-wrought exile, the sign that he has come to himself is that from all these wanderings of the thought he returns *home*.

Might we not, then, find place for more thorough study than people are apt to make, as to the duty and method of making homes and maintaining. homes, so that they may show the kingdom of God on earth most distinctly and most often? While you spend several years of a boy's life in teaching him how to write Greek badly, and how to write Latin badly, and how to speak French badly,— not forgetting the art of finding the greatest common denominator of two fractions,— might you not seriously and thoughtfully, as part of the regular training you give him, occupy his mind with thoughts and his life with habits which should tend directly and intentionally towards his power to make home happy, now he is a boy and when he shall be a man? People who make platform speeches or who write in the newspaper to show that women ought not to have the suffrage, spend much time in showing that it is women's business to make home happy. So it is. But it is just as much men's business to make home happy as it is the business of women. Of both, this is by far the most important business that they have in hand. Special political duties are as nothing; their special duties as church-members are as nothing; their success in their shops or at the bench is as nothing, compared with duty and success in making home to be bright and happy as the very kingdom of the Living God.

And I take this occasion to speak of this paramount duty, not so much because I expect in half an hour to go into the details of a duty to which, as I say, all life should be given, as because I think I can, in half an hour, point out some of the tendencies of modern life which confound us and thwart us in the discharge of these duties regarding home.

For there are two diverse temptations pressing us always. On the one hand, the individualizing folly of our time, and the pretence that a man is to live for himself alone and to die for himself alone, hurts homes, and turns men away from their duties there. And quite on the other side of the dial-plate, all theories of communism or socialism which want to reform the human race *en masse* have a tendency, in their way, also to discourage the simple and matter-of-fact people who find heaven nearest, and God, in the comforts of their own fireside.

I. Of the first of these two follies, I speak more briefly. A thoughtful, conscientious boy leaves his old home in the country, and comes to live his life-work in Boston. Let us suppose it is not very hard work. He is to be at the office at eight every morning,— he is to do what he is told to do,— he is to put things up when the firm go away,— to lock up at half-past three,— and then he is free. " Bed-time need not come till eleven," he says; "and here are seven hours and a half all my own. No wood to split, no horses or cows to feed, no children to bother me, no neighbors to come in and talk. Seven and a half hours to read, to go to

5

the theatre, to practise on the piano, to do just what I choose." An account almost boundless to draw upon, in the bank almost infinite of a boy's resources for amusement, pleasures, and life!

Yes; and I know nothing pleasanter than to see that fine young fellow the first evening he spends at the reading-room, or the second. I like to see him dip into the *Spectator* or the *Graphic*, and even try his maiden French on some French review. Nay, it is worth while to see him in his modest seat at the theatre, the first night he goes, or the second; well worth while to see his interest when he first hears a noble chorus or a perfect solo at the Music Hall. But when Music Hall, theatre, and reading-room are each an old story to him,—when he has to try hard to persuade himself that this lonely enjoyment of entertainment, provided by method and vote for him, makes up as "good a time" as came, without being provided, by the great open fireplace at home,—when I see that sense coming over my boy's face and life, then I see that he too is learning that no man lives for himself and no man dies for himself. I see he is learning the folly of mere self-culture, the folly of mere self-amusement, the folly of mere self in any form. In an experience as simple as that, he has learned, even granting that he has been tempted into no excesses and has drifted into no vices,—he has learned that for enjoyment, for culture, and for all true life, there is no place like Home. And I think one of the most charming things you see in life, is the fond effort such a youngster makes to reproduce home within the four walls of his lodging-room; when he begins to hang his pictures there, and to determine that it shall not look like a barrack; when he cares for the books on the table, for the neatness of the arrangement, and for anything else by which he may please some other lonely boy, and invite him in, that they may spend one evening, not in the reading-room, not at the Union, not at the theatre, but in a place which seems like home. The sweet potato badly baked in the embers, or the oysters stewing and burning a little on the hob, in a boy's poor efforts at cookery, all speak well for the exile who, with the meanest resources, is trying to provide himself a home.

Anthony Trollope, for whose philosophy I have a higher respect than most of my friends have, says in one of the best of his novels, that those people rate high among the practical saints, who are willing to welcome such exiled boys, lost in the wilderness of London, to the privilege of an evening visit in a cheerful London home. And he says that father or mother sending a boy into such exile may well bless and pray for the saints in the simplest London home, who will give such a welcome to their child.

II. Take that as an illustration of the dangers which, in the modern habits of life, threaten home-life, in separating boys and girls, even men and women, from the homes in which they belong. It is impossible to overstate that danger. But the other danger presses even more severely. It comes in, in our passion to do things on the large scale. We are really tempted to think that just as a railroad corporation can carry freight and passengers better than a man driving a horse, so we can contrive great organizations, which shall do the work of home better than the father, the mother, and the child can.

In my youth I had the great pleasure of a somewhat intimate acquaintance with Robert Owen, the socialist, the founder of New Lanark,— a communist experiment quite famous sixty or seventy years ago. For the purposes of New Lanark it was thought necessary to have women working in the cotton-mills, as, indeed, it is apt to be thought, in all cotton-mills. Of course, if women are working in cotton-mills they cannot be taking care of their babies at home. Robert Owen recognized this, and boldly said that it was much better that they should not. He said that they did not know how to take care of their children, and that it was much better that people who did should take care of them. Dr. Pestalozzi and his system of infant schools were much in fashion just then; and, as it was supposed, that Dr. Pestalozzi and Robert Owen together certainly knew more about the management of children than any single mother of a family could know, it was supposed that these poor babies would all be better off, if at birth they were sent to an infant-school together, while their mothers could then all be released to do their part in that great triumph of the nineteenth century, the manufacture of cotton cloth at lower rates than were ever known before. Such an infant-school was established, therefore, in the village of New Lanark,— a place which many excellent people really thought was the beginning of the kingdom of heaven among men. And when I last saw Robert Owen, which was when he was seventy-four years old and I was twenty-three, he really supposed that long before this year 1879, every baby in Christendom would be taken by law from its mother's arms to be educated in the most approved fashion under his system of infant-schools.

No burlesque or exaggeration could make these plans any more absurd than they were, as propounded by the people who believed in them. Fortunately, they were absurd enough to be their own immediate ruin. But, all the same, there lingers the wish to transfer from home life and home training both pleasures and duties which belong to them; in a hope encouraged by most of the prejudices of our time, that large organizations, because they are large, will do everything better than small organizations, because these are small.

Our great public-school system, for instance, because it is large, is blindly requested to accept and discharge duties which belong at home, and for which home has all the advantages. You are told that a public-school teacher ought to train her children in good manners. So she ought, if they are unmannerly. But the home is disgraced which has sent unmannerly children to school. It is precisely as the public school is made to teach the children to sew,— not because that is a good place for them to learn, but because this teaching is neglected at home, which is the best place to learn. So you find your boys unhandy : they cannot drive a nail or push a plane, as every Yankee boy could do a hundred years ago, and you are forced to propose industrial schools where boys shall be taught to use a hammer and a screw-driver. We had an intelligent and accomplished lady come to our church a few years ago and spend an hour and a half in explaining to us that there ought to be colleges for women, in which they should be taught how to make bread, how to broil a steak, and even how to amuse a child, and how to set a table. As if there were any place where a girl could learn any such thing, nearly as well as she could learn it, if she chose, under the humblest roof in America ! This all belongs to the passion for doing things on a large scalè, as the people of one country town are proud because their population is five thousand, and think the people of Nazareth hard by are disgraced because their population is only three thousand. And the habit shows itself, perhaps in its most painful form, when you are finally told that you must provide amusements on a large scale for jaded children, because their home pleasures do not satisfy them nov

Where it is true that you ought to do this,— and it sometimes is true,— it is because you are dealing with the lowest
and most degraded social orders. When you do have to
provide for the Wednesday and Saturday half-holiday of a
horde of children, when you have to see that their evenings
are spent in your chapel lest they should be wasted in riot
in your streets, it is because you are dealing with the most
degraded orders of human society. For substantial amusement, as well as for fundamental education, it is true that
there is no place like home.

III. So essential are such influences of home, for the
formation of all character, that they are to be considered
gravely in legislation, and in all other social economy. In
the Swiss system of watch-making, the workman does his
part at home, and brings it to the shop, where it is fitted to
other parts which have been made in other homes. In the
American system, the workman and the workwoman come to
the shop to work their ten hours, leaving their children to
the chances of the district school. The American system
may prove the best for watches,— but the Swiss system is the
best for children. It is said that in old Paris, the ingenious
French artisan lived near the place of his work, near the
shop where his work was sold. The artisans of Paris were
scattered in all parts of Paris. It is said that the immense
avenues and boulevards of the third Napoleon drove men
from such homes, to live together as they could in crowded
barracks on Montmartre and in Belleville. It is said that
to such crowding we owe the excesses and madness of the
Commune. I am not certain as to the facts; but from such
facts, whenever they are true, such a result must follow.
So you would find it hard to improve the condition, for
health, for morals, and for personal culture, of the New
England family of half a century ago, where every boy and
every girl had home work to do,— at the wheel, at the loom,
in the barn, in the wood-shed, in the dairy, or in the
kitchen,— by any of the devices of the over-praised division
of labor. And all such considerations are to be borne in
mind in all legislation which affects the condition of labor.

For myself, I have little doubt that the greatest political
question of all, the question on which government rests, will
be decided by reference direct to the home. I do not
believe that the suffrage, in the long run, will be conceded
to every man over twenty-one years of age. Our American

experiment in this line is a novelty, and a novelty not remarkably successful. Nor do I believe that the suffrage is to be doled out by property as it used to be in England, and was for centuries in Rome. The suffrage belongs to those who have a vital interest in the preservation of the social or organic life of the State; who have something to lose if the State is badly ruled. That is to say, the suffrage belongs especially to people who have established homes; and it is my belief that to a homestead suffrage the free nations of the world will ultimately recur.

IV. Now, when we apply to all this the eternal question, " What shall we do about it?" the immediate answer is, that all of us, children as well as men and women, are to make home as happy as we can, so that it may be as strong as may be against whatever counter-poises or counter-powers threaten it in our times. That was a wise remark of a wise woman, who said she counted the battle of life won, if, at fifteen, her children preferred their home to any other place in the world,— a remark not true without exceptions, but to be trusted a great way. Now, you do not get such homes as that involves by singing " Sweet Home " in chorus, by listening to sermons about home, or, in general, without some effort,— yes, and some sacrifice. Are you willing to teach your own boys and girls to play whist at home? or do you prefer to go to the club to play a much better game with much better players? There is a test question. Are you willing to read " Ivanhoe " to those two children, instead of leaving them to read " Red as a Rose is She," while you go to the theatre to see Sara Bernhardt? That is a test question. Do you really think the happiness of home a matter so central that it shall very largely regulate the expenditure of your money and of your time? That is the question which all discussion of the place of home comes round to.

In my boyhood there were two characters in fiction, who, though they had no names, as it happened, still had great influence on all young people. I wish I thought they were as well-known to the rising generation of to-day. One of them was called " Frank's father," and the other was named " Frank's mother." Other names they had none. It was Frank's father who said that he had rather teach his own son to ride than have him taught by any servant in his employ. He said he fairly coveted the pleasure of knowing that, in after life, his son should always associate the pleasure of riding on horseback with his father and with his home. In that remark lies a central truth, and that example is well worth following.

That remark carries us far into the whole difficult question as to amusement. The German household at Berlin or Weimar, seeking its entertainment for the afternoon or the evening, goes *together* to the music-garden. The home type is preserved. Grandfather and grandmother and grandchildren, down to babies in arms, share in the recreation. The elders sit round the tables ; the young people walk or play in the garden alleys, and listen to Strauss's band the while. Compare that — nay, let me hope that you do not know how to compare it — with an American variety-hall, where are four or five hundred men and boys sitting by themselves, without the presence, perhaps, of a single woman, and certainly without the presence of a child. In all the discussions of the last twenty years as to the amusements of the people, the only point fairly wrought out is this : that you must respect family life in your public amusement as in everything beside. Do not let your amusement be the means of separating father from mother, children from parents, or parents from children. You have no method so sure for maintaining the purity of such entertainment as in consecrating it by the purity of home.

All boys and girls, as they grow up, suppose, I think, that this undefined charm of home comes quite of course, and that nobody has cared for it or has thought of it. If it is not around their young lives, the poor creatures hardly know what they have lost. If it is around them, they take it without a thought, — as they take health and air and sunshine. What I am saying, I am saying to such boys and girls to remind them that this is not of course. The home is wretched where the father appears only for a hurried meal, while he seeks his life elsewhere ; or from which the mother escapes as if it were a pest-house, leaving her children to themselves or to her servants. If home is the kingdom of God, — and the kingdom of God home may be, — it is because the spirit of God is there. It is because the woman who is the queen of that home makes home the centre of her thought, her hope, and her prayer ; it is because the man who has sworn to love her, to honor her, and to cherish her knows that he but keeps his oath by making her home and his home glad, cheerful, and beautiful because he does not neglect it and desert it. To those two there grow up children

who know that the noblest duty is the duty next their hand ;
who are glad to surprise their mother with a new pleasure, or
to relieve her from some old care ; children who find their
father their best companion, and who have no secret from
him of boyhood's or of girlhood's joys or sorrows. The
original trinity — the trinity from which all scholastic and
ecclesiastical trinities were borrowed — is the sacred trinity
of the father, the mother, and the child,— one in three, and
three in one. It is a life undivided, a life only perfect when
each shares with each, each is intertwined with each, and
each sustains all, " that they may be made perfect in one."

In the last interview of the Saviour with the twelve, at
the moment when he drew farthest the veil which separated
this world from the other, he did so by saying: "In my
father's house are many homes." This phrase most precisely expresses his meaning, which the stately word "man-
sion" of our Bibles hardly conveys. Heaven, when we pass
from earth, will be a life of homes. Not in one utterance,
but in a hundred, has he made the other statement, which
is the converse of this: We need not wait till we die to
enter that heaven. No ! the kingdom of heaven is at hand ;
it is here and now. Faith, hope, and love, the greatest of
the three, make heaven, wherever faith and hope and love
combine ; and to man, or woman, or child, there is a present certainty and present enjoyment of the very heaven of
God,— he does not say a foretaste of it. he says there is
the present reality,— in a faithful, hopeful, loving Home.

From Thanksgiving to Fast.

FIFTEEN SERMONS

BY

EDWARD E. HALE.

THE GREAT HARVEST YEAR,
LOOKING BACK,
RITUAL,
PRAYER,
RESPECTABILITY,
YOURSELVES,
WHAT IT IS TO BE CATHOLIC,
THE JOY OF LIFE,
THE ASSOCIATED CHARITIES,
THE REVISION OF THE BIBLE,
THE BIBLE,
LENT,
NEW LIFE,
BLASPHEMY AGAINST THE HOLY GHOST,
THE FUTURE OF NEW ENGLAND.

Price in paper covers, $1.00; in cloth binding, $1.25.

A second series (of fifteen) of Mr. Hale's sermons is now being issued, of which there have already been printed

THE LIFE IN COMMON,
BODY, MIND, AND SOUL,
BODILY TRAINING,
MENTAL DISCIPLINE,
CANDOR IN THE PULPIT,
SPIRITUAL EXERCISES,
DAILY BREAD,
HAPPY HOMES.

Price, 10 cents per copy, or $1.00 for the series. Published
GEO. H. ELLIS, 101 Milk Street, Boston.

DAILY BREAD.

A SERMON

PREACHED AT SAGE CHAPEL, CORNELL UNIVERSITY,

OCTOBER 29, 1879,

BY

EDWARD E. HALE.

BOSTON:

GEO. H. ELLIS, PRINTER, 101 MILK STREET.

1879.

PRESS OF GEO. H. ELLIS, 101 MILK STREET.

DAILY BREAD.

Give us this day our daily bread.—MATTHEW VI., 11.

I suppose that these are the first words of the Lord's
Prayer which little children understand, after the words
"Our Father." They are undoubtedly the first ones about
which they question.

"How is it, mamma, that God gives us daily bread, when
we know it is bought in the shop, or that it is in the house
while we are offering our prayer?" The questioning is not
theirs only. You meet men and women, not irreligious
either, who are puzzled about prayer for bodily gifts. "God
has adjusted the laws of matter," they say. "He is not
going to change them at our suggestion. It is the laws of
spirit on which our spirits joined with his can act," they say.
Let our petitions, then, they say, be only those for spiritual
blessings. I once knew a student of divinity who was so
far impressed by this line of reasoning, that in his public
services he omitted this petition from the Lord's Prayer.
This reformer of the New Testament did not remain long in
the Christian ministry. But I think he expressed an uncer-
tainty which many Christians feel.

If we had come here to philosophize this afternoon, the
consideration of such difficulties would open for us the
whole tempting subject of the relation of spirit and matter.
What is matter and what is spirit? What are spiritual laws,
and what are material? Where does the attractive power
which, as the hymn says, "holds the drops that sparkle in
the shower, and the planets in their force," cease to be a law
of matter; and where does the law of love begin which, as
the same hymn says, "attaches soul to soul"? Are these
one law, as the Swedenborgians say? Or, put the question
as Dr. Bellows puts it ingeniously: Are our souls in our
bodies, as the usual speech of men implies, or are our bodies
in our souls, as some stubborn facts seem to say they are?

But we have not come here to philosophize, and I do not
therefore enter on these tempting questions. They have

been at issue since the world began ; and it is so far probable that in twenty minutes we· might not decide them, that I
had rather examine the petition for daily bread in its simplicity. We will try to find how we are to offer it in our
daily prayer, and how much Jesus meant it should comprehend.

I. I must observe first, that as Jesus uttered the prayer it
carried a meaning much wider than the literal words convey.
How wide that meàning went, indeed, it is hard to tell. A
translation nearly literal would be : " Give us this day the
bread of our being"; and any difficulty which would attach to
the interpretation of that phrase attaches equally to the
words in the original. It was by the boldest paraphrase
only that the words "*daily* bread " were used in our translation. We are to remember, then, as we discuss the phrase,
that they are to be construed in their very widest range. We
ask God in this prayer to give us this day all that we need in ·
order that we may *be*. We do not ask simply for the bread
which supports the body; we do not ask simply for material
out of which to assimilate the constituents of blood and
nerves and muscles : we ask for all possible food which feeds
the man. The Saviour, who has taught us that man does not
live by bread alone,— teaching it, indeed, in the signal moment of his own victory,— does not mean that we shall pray
merely for meat and drink. " Man does not live by bread
alone, but by every word that proceedeth from the mouth of
God doth he live," he says. Thus he extends and glorifies
the words which Moses used with a lesser significance. So
as I come to God at daybreak, and say to him: Father, give
us this day our daily bread, I ask — yes — for the provision
which will support this body that it may not faint ; but I ask
for much more : I ask for food for this mind that it may not
feed upon itself, and I merely turn over and over what I
learned yesterday, the day before, and last year. Not
only this, but I ask for much more. Body and mind are only
two little slaves of the soul, where the soul knows her power.
The soul says : " Do this," and they do it ; " Go there," and
they go ; " Abstain," and they abstain, though the tempting
morsel be at the lip. The little hound is held in the leash,
though the startled game flutters before his eye. For this
soul we pray, centre and lord of being : " Father, that thou·
wilt feed my soul ; give love the fit food for love, give hope
the fit food for hope, give faith the fit food for faith. That
which it must have, which thou, O God, knowest so much

better than I,— the essential necessity of its being,— be pleased this day to give my soul."

II. "I can join in that last petition," says timid faith to me. "I can understand that God is the father of my soul, feeds my soul. Nay, I understand that by his immutable laws he is the author of my body, and feeds my body. But my trouble is, that I have no right to pray to him to-day to meet my *bodily* wants. If the laws of Nature, which he has established for seed-time and harvest, will feed me, I need not pray for other laws. If they will not feed me, I dare not ask him to change them simply to serve my turn."

Let me confess to timid faith like this,— that this diffi- culty has been always felt. The early fathers, in concession to it, construed this prayer as having reference simply to the soul's necessities. If God did not choose to feed the body, they said, of his own unsolicitcd will, let the body go.

But let me declare at the same moment that it is a difficulty which I do not feel. I have said I would not try to define the world of spirit and the world of matter. I will not. I will not try to show where the laws of matter end and the laws of spirit begin ; though I do think that discus- sion will help timid faith in this matter. Leaving that discussion, I had rather meet timid faith on its own ground. For I think we may show that the laws of spirit have by far the most to do in the supply even of our bodily wants. I think we can show this of what everybody admits to be laws of spirit. Let alone the questions regarding God's fixed purposes for matter. Let us see how our bodily lives hinge on his spiritual laws, on the growth or failure of other living souls, which he cares for and which he moves. And for this, we will not begin with the broadest view of this petition, but with the most literal and narrow. I will take the familiar definitions in the most familiar illustrations. I will take the illustration of the child's question regard- ing this prayer. The loaf of bread on your table to-morrow morning ; how does that come to you ? Does it come from these unchanging material laws, or does it come from these spiritual interpositions of the present love of God which you are willing to acknowledge ? Do you hastily reply that it is the material product of material agencies, that it comes chiefly from seed-corn, sunshine, moisture, and the darkness of the earth ; that beside these the waterfall has ground it, the leaven has leavened it, and the fire has baked

it, by laws which God impressed on them all in the beginning? I will not parry your declaration even by asking what
you mean by "in the beginning" in speaking of God, who
has no beginning and no end,— to whom this period since
his spirit breathed upon the waters and he said, "Let there be
light," up to this instant, is indeed nothing. Yet I might do
that fairly. I had rather leave philosophy so profound. I
had rather look at the immediate fact to which you appeal,—
the fact of the kitchen, of the grain-market, and of the Western harvest. Is this loaf of bread the product of material
agencies merely? All the material agencies you name were
here three centuries ago. The sun shone as kindly, the dews
fell as softly, the prairie was as rich, the waterfall was as strong,
the fire was as warm. What, then, if some centuries ago Sir
Philip Sidney had landed on our coast, as he wanted to, and
had sought this fruit of your material laws? Would he have
found it,— would he have found anything to compare with
it? He would have found, if he had searched long enough,
a few handfuls of savages lurking in the wilderness, dying
faster than their children were born, because these material
laws of yours did not give them their daily bread! He
would have found that peninsula which we call New England the lair of about twenty thousand of these starving
human brutes, fighting for a sustenance which they could
not find. He would have found the State of Vermont, for
instance, without one human inhabitant, for the simple reason that the material laws you tell me of did not supply
the physical daily bread which would keep one human being
living there the year round.

"Oh, I grant," you say, "that men must use these material laws; nay, that civilized men must use them." Do you
grant that? Granting that, you grant everything. For the
moment man comes in, the child of God comes in; the
moment he appears, the laws of spirit are working with
the laws of matter; and the moment civilized man comes in,
there comes in man in whom spiritual law has gained the
mastery over carnal law, and so works its triumphs most
completely.

And, for my illustration, I do not care whether the wheat
of your loaf came from your own rich valley, — from Genesee
County, or from a prairie a thousand miles away. The courage which sent the first Daniel Boone or the first Manasseh
Cutler to that prairie was a spiritual gift founded on spiritual
law, sustained, most likely,— like all courage which is good for

much,— on profound faith in the Great Spirit of all. And come down to this *day* — the " this day " of the prayer. The perseverance which ploughed that prairie last October, and the industry which reaped it this summer, are not material agencies, but spiritual powers. They are powers which are weak and mean when the man hardly lives. They are powers which are strong and dignified in proportion as the man gains life. They are strongest and noblest when he gains life most abundantly. So of the ingenuity which contrived the reaping-machine which cut that harvest, or which built the mill which ground it, or which devised the engine which dragged it night and day from the garner to your home, or the iron road on which it sped along on that journey of blessing. Industry, perseverance, wit, and ingenuity like these were not physical powers like the power which speeds the falling apple. You do not find that a stout New Zealander has them in proportion as he is strong and tall. You do not find that they grow as man grows in weight or in muscle. They are spiritual gifts,— not the highest yet, but children of the highest; and they have never existed where the highest spiritual gifts were not near at hand. Nor am I afraid to speak here of those highest gifts of all,— of conscience, of prayer, of long-suffering,— nay, of martyrdom,— which must be before your daily bread is upon your board. Only I declare I do not know what instances to select out of a million. The mother who sits in the sickly log-cabin on the prairie, making it the cheerful home of her husband, who is toiling in the field for you,— she is preserving his life for him, though her own ebbs away in the midst of malaria and of care which is too much for her. She is not making that place a home, and giving him the courage for his daily labor. because she is a piece of clock-work wrought by physical law, And the men whose courage and conduct deliver, day by day, at your Western ports, the bread for the nation in each day's labor,— they would not work up to that mark for any mere bribe of silver that you could offer them. Vouch for that for me ; you who direct these packets and railroads, and receive their supplies. Own to me that you have no physical system of checks and balances, no book-keeping, no accounting nor oversight, which saves you from the necessity of employing *honest men*. Pearls beyond price indeed, which the merchantman seeks for now as in the Lord's parable. Bear testimony for me again, you bankers, that if every man who had the accounts of these great enterprises to hold were a man without spiritual power, without integrity, without honor, without sense of right and wrong, had as little spiritual power as a Tweed or a Sweeney, those proud works would crumble into decay, as not whirlwind nor deluge could overthrow them. Yes, and go farther yet: ask about these giant works,— your steam-engines and your telegraphs. The men who invent them, who compel an unwilling people to build these avenues of your trade,— the men over whose work is rolled along every day the daily bread that our Father gives to us,— are not men who are ruled by physical laws, or whose triumph is a physical triumph. They are not compassing wealth ; they do not seek it, and they do not gain it. They compel you to do that which they see can be done ; they subdue the earth as they set out to do, and then their great mission is fulfilled,— when the East and West are brought together,— and they step aside and die unhonored and forgotten. It is not such a law as the attraction of gravitation, merely, that creates your Western harvest. It is not such a law as the laws of tides or of eclipses that brings it to your door. It is the soul's life which has sent it,— nay, and God created it ; it is industry, devotion, and hope ; it is integrity ; it is public spirit ; it is manliness and faith. To agencies like these, God-given and God-sustained, acting in a million hearts and ruling a million of lives, is it that, as we live, you owe every day every crust of your daily bread.

And I state this so briefly, only as the humblest instance, in the most casual matter, of a great reality. We are not in any moment dependent chiefly or largely on what we are pleased to call the laws of matter. We are all girt in by spiritual powers. It is love that feeds us, it is faith that feeds us, it is hope that feeds us. If these spiritual powers should cease for an instant, it would be worse for us than deluge, worse than total eclipse, worse than the crash of planet against planet in the Empyrean. We could not live as stones exist, or as the waters roll. Not we ! For we are his children. We are infinite beings. It is not of the earth that we live, nor by the earth that we are fed. It is in God that we live, in God that we move, and in God that we have our being.

III. Of the immediate bearing of this great truth on our petition, I shall speak again. But let me first stop to remind you that there is another necessity of the petition,— when we only think of ourselves who utter it. And here, as before, I

find it most simple not to take the broadest meaning of the
text, but only the child's notion. The loaf of bread is in the
house, the child says. Yes. It is on the table, perhaps.
Yes. But is the way from the loaf to the lip so certain?
Were you never at the table, with the bounty of God ready
spread, at the culmination of all those infinite mercies which
have tended to that moment of your life, when of an instant
you found that that bread was not for you? You only broke
the seal of a letter, and lo! there was the message within
which made you and yours forget food that day. Or a messenger came running to the door, or there was a cry of agony
from up-stairs,— nay, a thankless child at the board beside
you spoke one hateful word,— and you pushed the ready
bread away. It was not for you! No; man does not live
by such bread alone. Cannot live by it, unless he have —
oh, how many mercies from the mouth of God! And so
again is it that no man dare say he stands. No man dare
count on to-morrow, nor *this day*. No man dare say, "I
have provided. This hour is mine." But at every moment
of his life man may well entreat God to overrule still the
courses of the world which are inwoven with his destiny,
and in whatever little prudence or providence of his own to
murmur, " Give us this day our daily bread."

IV. Now let us try, with such help as these two little
illustrations give us, to open out some of the wider range of
the import of these seven words of prayer. We see that
unless we live ourselves we cannot receive our daily bread.
We must be well enough to receive it, our friends must be
well enough, all around us well enough, lest this be a feast of
. Tantalus which we have provided, and vanish at the moment
when we sit for the banquet. Yes, and we see also that not
only must we provide, as we say so proudly, but God must
keep up a million agencies now at work in full force for us, or
we cannot provide,— agencies not of matter only, as a world
fond of stones and bricks is used to say, but of the highest,
tenderest spiritual laws.
And if this is true in these little carnal necessities from
which muscles are fed and blood set flowing, how much more
of all the other necessities of our lives! Now let me go
back of the child's conception of the prayer. Let me speak
of it as Jesus used it. Give us that which is essential
for our being. We do not pray to God as if we were only
so much muscle, vein, and artery. We do not simply say,

"Keep this blood flowing, keep these nerves thrilling": we pray to him as those who remember, reflect, and plan for the future. So we pray that our Father will keep this mind unshaken, these memories true, and these plans coherent. Feed them, O Father, with food sufficient for them. Nay, we pray as those who love him and love each other; who believe in him and in each other; who hope nothing less than heaven for ourselves and for each other. Feed these longings, these appetites divine, great God, lest we cease to love, to hope, or to believe. And this is not for *me*, but for *us*; not for *my* daily bread, but for *ours*. So be pleased, great God, to all of us to give the waters divine, of which if one drink he never thirsts; the bread of life, of which if one eats he never dies. Not for me only, but for my brothers and sisters,— all my brothers, all my sisters. Feed the body, feed the mind,— yes, this day, Father,— and so much more the soul, with this daily bread, this essential food of its necessity; with the revelation of thyself and of thine own loving kindness, of thine own tender help here and of thine own sweet will; with all fond hopes, loving affections; with all tender mercies; with all certainty of thine own help and comfort and blessing. Feed us all, great God, so that we may grow in grace, fed by the abundance of thy love; so that we may more truly live; so that we may the better pray, and to-morrow shall utter one prayer something closer to thee than ever, when we say: —

> Our Father who art in heaven,
> Hallowed be thy name.
> Thy kingdom come,
> Thy will be done on earth as it is in heaven.

For this be pleased to feed us, Father,— body, mind, and soul. So be pleased, then, to

> Give us — even this day — our daily bread.

From Thanksgiving to Fast.

FIFTEEN SERMONS

BY

EDWARD E. HALE.

THE GREAT HARVEST YEAR,
LOOKING BACK,
RITUAL,
PRAYER,
RESPECTABILITY,
YOURSELVES,
WHAT IT IS TO BE CATHOLIC,
THE JOY OF LIFE,
THE ASSOCIATED CHARITIES,
THE REVISION OF THE BIBLE,
THE BIBLE,
LENT,
NEW LIFE,
BLASPHEMY AGAINST THE HOLY GHOST,
THE FUTURE OF NEW ENGLAND.

Price in paper covers, $1.00; in cloth binding, $1.25.

A second series (of fifteen) of Mr. Hale's sermons is now being issued, of which there have already been printed

THE LIFE IN COMMON,
BODY, MIND, AND SOUL,
BODILY TRAINING,
MENTAL DISCIPLINE,
CANDOR IN THE PULPIT,
SPIRITUAL EXERCISES,
DAILY BREAD.

Price, 10 cents per copy, or $1.00 for the series. Published by GEO. H. ELLIS, 101 Milk Street, Boston.

THE SEVENTY RETURNED.

A SERMON

PREACHED AT THE SOUTH CONGREGATIONAL CHURCH,
BOSTON, NOV. 9, 1879,

BY

EDWARD E. HALE.

BOSTON:

GEORGE H. ELLIS, 101 MILK STREET.

1879.

PRESS OF GEO. H. ELLIS, 101 MILK STREET.

THE SEVENTY RETURNED.

And the seventy returned with joy.— LUKE x., 17.

It was the simplest system of missions that the world ever saw. If any two people took any real interest in the ·new kingdom, they were sent out to interest other people. They were not asked to profess their faith, or to account for it, or to justify it ; but they were told to show it ; and, which is to be carefully noticed also, they were sent out two and two. They were not sent alone.

I dare say a great many were disgusted at being sent away. They wanted to. sit at a Saviour's feet, and anoint them with ointment ; they wanted to have him comfort them and teach them more ; in some cases they selfishly wanted offices near his person. They were so much like people now, that I dare say a great many of them thought they would like to spend all their time in conversing about the kingdom of God. It is a great deal easier to converse about it than to bring it in.

But that was not his way,— is not his way. He sent them away, two by two, just as soon as they had any notion about the kingdom, to try the vital experiment whether the new-planted seed had any root ; whether they had any real and vital faith.

The system, you see, took care of itself. If they were disgusted, and went home, one to his farm and another to his merchandise, why they went, that was all. They did not have to be taken off any list of the Church, because they had never been put on. There was no list. On the other hand, if they worked for the kingdom, they gained new light and new life as to what it was. They did not have to be put upon any list of the Church, because their zeal and activity kept it always evident that they were the Master's men.

And, when they had discharged any special duty, they came back to him. It is this habit and this part of the plan which occupies us to-day. They had the responsibility of duty on

4

the one hand,— yes, and they had the comfort and rest of
conference with him on the other.

They came back once in great spirits. They had had such
success as was marvellous. The possessed people, up and
down Galilee, had yielded to them, just as they did to him.
" Why, dear Master, even the devils are subject to us, through
thy name ! " I am afraid that his answer is often miscon-
ceived. Not without sympathy, yet with anxiety, which has
been wholly justified in the history of his Church,— he
warned them against the danger of just such boasting, of the
vanity or the pride belonging to it. Woe to the messenger,
indeed, who thinks more of himself than of his errand ! And,
in his reply, he reminded them how, in the Jewish mythol-
ogy, Satan — almost the noblest of God's servants once — fell
from heaven, because of his pride in his own power. ". Do
not rejoice," he said, " because spirits are subject to you.
Rejoice that your names are written in heaven." And, just
cautioning them thus gently, he rejoiced in spirit : "I thank
Thee, Father, that having hidden these things from the wise
and prudent, Thou hast revealed them unto babes." It is
worth remark that Shakspere reverts to this lesson in that
celebrated warning of his against personal ambition, where
Wolsey says : —

" Cromwell, I charge thee fling away ambition.
By that fault fell the angels."

Then there is the outbreak of those who came back, and
had denounced one who was preaching alone, and did not
choose to walk with them,— perhaps would not come back to
the Master with them, or as they did. " He was casting out
devils in thy name, and we forbade him, because he followed
not with us."
" No, do not forbid him. No man can do a miracle in my
name, and lightly speak evil of me."
This unknown disciple is, justly enough, a person of great
interest to all of us free lances and liberals. Jesus' treatment
of him is perfectly in character. And one dares not say that
this man, who is the typical representative of the " Come-
outer," though he did not choose to add himself to one of
the regular parties who prided themselves on their Orthodoxy had not for his own comfort his own fashion of
coming back to his Master for sympathy and instruction.

They came back once in great spirits again; and he asked them about the popular report concerning him : " Whom do men say that I am ? "

" Oh, some say John the Baptist, and some Elijah, and some do not know which prophet, but know it is a prophet — that one of the old prophets is risen again." It would be a good picture,— the eagerness and pride on their faces, and the amused sympathy on his. " Yes ; and who do you say that I am ? " How should they answer,— with a name as great as Elijah's name ? How can they say that he is greater than John — the controller and master of the people ? How shall they say, that they have found out, in the heart of their hearts, that he brings that which Elijah never brought, and to which John never pretended ? A pause of a minute, broken then by Simon Peter, with the audacity that belongs to genius,— yes, and the genius that inspires audacity,— in the simple words which have become the greatest in language, simple because great, great because simple ; which express enough, and do not express too much ; and which were all the more great and the more fit for his purpose, because they were not taken from the old books, and did not refer specifically to them ; — we forget they had not been said before,—

" Thou art the Christ, the Son of the Living God."

" Well-said, Peter ; flesh and blood has not revealed this to you, but my Father who is in heaven."

To send them out, two by two to work, with the idea that they would recur to him for comfort, rest, instruction, sympathy ; that was the whole plan — is the whole plan. All the rest of the mission and ministry organization of the Christian Church is surplusage, matter of convenience or temporary arrangement. This is the whole plan as he laid it down.

The apostles followed in it, after his death, as they did before. Paul would go off with Barnabas, or Barnabas with Mark, or Paul with Silas, or Aquila with his wife Priscilla ; they would cast out such devils as they found, would teach such inquirers as they met, would comfort those that were cast down wherever they were ; and yet all along they were coming back to get his help, his wish, his inspiration. Where they should find him was never a question to them. They believed absolutely in the "two or three" doctrine. " Where two or three are gathered together in my name, I am in the midst of them." Paul would sometimes go back to Jerusalem to meet the brethren there. He would sometimes go back to Corinth to meet the handful there, or at the communion table, whenever he could meet with two or three, or with more of those who loved the memories of Jesus' life, he was sure to find his Spirit there.

Did none of the preachers or missionaries ever go off and work on their own basis, refusing to come back to him? Of course they did. "Demas hath forsaken me," said Paul, when for once he found himself without the companion in travel whom he was used to have. And from Demas's time down to this time, there has been many a man, who, finding out that the Spirit of God was speaking in his words, and helping him in his life, has gone off from the Saviour who first opened his heart to the Spirit of God, and has been proud enough, or vain enough, as you may choose to call it, self-poised, self-sustained enough, to make his own proclamation afterwards, without trying to come back to the Saviour's side to light again his torch, or to renew his inspiration. But what difference does this make to the whole? If what these men say or do is true, it stands; if it is not true, it falls. Practically, what is apt to happen is what happened to Satan. He fell from heaven so soon as his own pride overmastered him. Of Jesus Christ, the great victory was, that he made himself of no reputation. To such independents the only danger comes when they make themselves of a great deal of reputation. But, as I say, the end is all the same. What they say of truth lives. What they say that is merely personal, or what is not true, dies. And so with other rubbish, that history casts off year after year, are the names of a good many self-worshipping prophets. But, among the diamonds which shine all the brighter, because dross and chaff which surrounded them are burned away, are the names of many a man who had his own way of casting out devils in Christ's name, though he did not follow in the standard-bearing regiment.

All this is just as true of our generation as it was of those early generations. And I do not need to apply it to preachers and missionaries and other people who have to do with the formal proclamation of Christianity; for at this moment I am not speaking to many of them. The application is just as important in those details of daily life and duty — all of them sacred — which occupy us who are here.

For the truth is that we are all sent out in little groups, with this same leaven, mustard-seed, spark of fire,— to do with it, in our several lives, what we can. And we are to do this together,— two and two, three and three; now in co-partnerships, now in families, you in a school-room, you in a law-office, you in the wards of a hospital, you in the market, you in the bank,— different scenes for all of us, but all of us together. The leaven is the simple word, " The kingdom of God is at hand,"— God's present power; yes, and his present love. And we are to see what we can do with that in buying, in selling, in making clothes and chairs and tables; in discounting bills, and borrowing money; in arguing cases, and dressing wounds; in teaching children their letters, in amusing them when they are sick; in planting gardens, in gathering fruit; in going to sea, in coming home from vacation, in furnishing our houses, and in living with our neighbors. There is a great deal of all this which seems very unlike the scenery of Nazareth, or Nain, or Gethsemane, or Bethany; and it will carry us into the midst of language and methods, which are not at all Oriental or Biblical,— where there is very little said about grace or faith, about parable or Saviour. None the less are we to carry into those scenes the holy secret of "the kingdom of God," and see what we can make of it. Jesus Christ has made the possibility of it real to us, and now we are to take the infinite secret with us, and find and show what value it has for the world!

Then those of us who choose can refuse to come back to the Saviour for farther light or other direction. We can thank him for his instructions, and say that we now understand the whole thing perfectly, and that we can do all that is to be done without ever consulting him again. That is just what boys who think well of themselves do sometimes, when they have got their first inkling of an art or science. " I am very much obliged to you. Now I understand it perfectly." I knew a young painter once, who said he should be ashamed to go to Italy to learn more of his art. He could teach himself, and would. But that young fool learned better. And in the second stage most of these adventurers who think they have learned the whole of the great science of life,— of the art of arts, which is the art of living,— most of them learn better. However it may be with them, the great majority of men and women who have learned anything at a Saviour's lips, or gained anything from his life, are glad to come back to him again and again, and yet again,

to compare their lives with his life, and to take what the
seamen call "a new departure."

What is most extraordinary is, that if people's lives
have been near the true plane, they find that his life in its
detail was so varied and so broad. that they can make the
direct comparison — life with life — theirs with his, if they
have been near the true plane. For instance ; you have been
spending this last week in reorganizing your home. You
have been dealing with servants who were willing enough, but
so dull. You wanted to be in ten places at a time. You
thought you explained yourself, and then it proved nobody
understood you. You thought that this and that had been
provided for, and then it proved that, because you had not
seen to it, everybody had neglected it. Ah well! Is this
your life only? Could I not have described that all in
Scripture language? Had not he to build up all his work
with just such agents? "Do ye not understand, neither
remember?" How that wail of his sounds like yours of yesterday! "How is it that you do not understand?" "And
they were afraid, and they asked him of this or that which
had been forty times explained to them." From all that
experiment of yours in life, if you come back to him, it is to
find that he made just the same experiment. And it is to
learn in what spirit he sustained such trials that you come
back to him.

Or you have been teaching children all the week. In the
primary school, or in one of the higher schools, you have
had to measure yourself against forty high-spirited, wide-
aawke lives, all quickened just now by the oxygen of the past
summer. If to-day were not Sunday, you would be engaging
every faculty of your being in sympathy with them, in
studying how to answer them, in working out the solution
to the infinite problems, as they propose them so frankly.
Thank God, it is Sunday! And you come back to him
to-day. To him ; to whom? Why, to *the* Teacher — the
Teacher of teachers — whose system is education in its
perfection, whose method is as completely the method of an
infant school as it is the method of the kingdom of God ;
for these two are one. No! Your primary school is quite
unlike anything which was ever seen in Capernaum. But
you find yourself no stranger when you come back to him.

And the same is true of you men who do in a day not one

thing, but a hundred. You do not know when you take your mail in hand in the morning what questions you will be asking or what interests deciding before noon. The man of business must be armed at all points, and ready to answer all questions. He must be, in the noble sense in which Paul was, all things to all men. He must be quick with the quick. He must be patient with the dull. He must explain to the ignorant; he must lead the blind; he must talk on his fingers even to the deaf. See how in such language I use almost unconsciously the very language in which the gospel describes Jesus Christ; and see how the man of affairs, if he will, may turn back to the life of him who really directs all business that is best carried on this day, to find that he knew in his own experience just that confusion and variety of incident, that turmoil of unexpected exigency which makes the wildest variety in our common duty.

See him, when every man around him is perplexing and thwarting him. See him when his friends and his enemies, those whom he trusted and those whom he distrusted, seem to stand apart from him, the one party as far as another. See him come from placid Galilee to stormy, quarrelsome Jerusalem; pass in a week from the calm of the one to the crisis, passion, chaos, of the other! It is not a chaos which is spoken of in any of our modern jargons; but the spirit of its surprises is just like ours: and the Spirit which walked serenely over the waters of those storms will walk as serenely over these!

Thus easy is it to come back to him, even with joy, as the seventy did, if your lives are near his plane. If your lives are near his plane. But suppose they are on another plane. Imagine the man, who in the turns of the exchange has not been caring for his workmen, for his friends, even for his honor, but only caring for himself. I have heard of men who sold their own honor, in the chance of affecting the stock-market so that they might profit,— men who are only to be compared to women who sell their honor for a place at court, or a showy dress, or a jewel. Imagine a man like that, on the morning of Sunday, as he sees his children finding their books for the Sunday-school, his wretched wife preparing herself for church,— imagine him with some lingering thoughts of boyhood, of purity, of what the church is built and the service meant for, trying to compare his life with his Saviour's life. Imagine him, after the family have left him at home, stealthily taking up the gilded Bible from the dusty table it lies upon, where it has lain since his grandmother gave it to him on his wedding-day. Imagine him reading through from Matthew to the end of John, that he may renew the life of lives, in his own memory, and find out what is the marvel which, to this hour, holds the world. Parables about sharpers? Yes! The money-changers driven out of the house of God? Yes. Rebuke to those who would buy their way into heaven? Yes! But in the Master's words, not one word he could have spoken himself as this week went by. In the kingdom of God with men, not one feature or element which has been in his crafty plans for these six days. Its love is world-wide from his cunning. Its freedom is so far apart from his slavery.

That man is no fool. And, as he reads, he may well understand what the outer darkness is of the selfish and unprofitable servant; for to that outer darkness he is himself consigned.

Yes, and we need not take our illustration from people who undergo what the world calls the great temptations,— the people who deal in a great deal of money; who, if they rise, are mentioned in the newspapers, or if they fall ruin thousands. The beggar in his hovel may be as selfish as the monarch on his throne. What man or what woman has lived, this week through, I do not say for wealth, but for self in any form; has daily fretted and fumed about the food on the table, flavors, cookery, selection; or has given the week to lonely and mean thoughts of dress or fashion; or has been carrying his own point or hers, over the heads of one, two, or three who were too proud or too pure for contention? Let that man or that woman try to come back and measure life against the Master's life. Ah! it is again to find that life needs a new departure indeed. To him or to her the gospel has but one word. Unless you can cut loose from the past, and for the future set your sail to another breeze, unless you can turn about and renew life, you cannot be my disciple.

What is the plane of my life? And how hard is it for me, or how easy, to come back to a Saviour's life, and from him to take counsel and example? Let me try the resemblance of life upon a comet, as it draws near to the sun, and then recedes. The people who live on such a comet are conscious for years upon years that their climate is improving. New forms of life and beauty develop there, as century follows after century. I have no doubt that the reformers on these comets think that the improvement is their own work, and point back to such a treatise or such a political victory as marking the epoch when crops began to improve, and life to be more delightful. But the angels who have charge of them smile, and understand that they are all the time coming nearer to the source of heat, from which, as God orders, their life and light and glory depend. Then they pass round the sun, for awhile enjoying the glories of a summer before unknown,— pass as near to it as our world passes, or one of the planets which are yet closer. And then the comet recedes. Men do not know it at first, but in truth that centre of light and heat is growing smaller and smaller. The gardening is less successful, the sub-tropical plants do not show so much color, the grain does not ripen. And at first people shut their eyes to the change. They abuse the ignorance of the gardener. They say it is all the fault of the stupidity of the farmer. Ah! all the same the real trouble is that there is less and less of the heat and light without which the gardener planted and the husbandman ploughed in vain! And we. It is easy,— it is very easy, to count success our own work. "I contrived this so nicely; I planned that so wisely." When we are working towards the light, and are at one with the infinite laws, success is certain. And we can persuade ourselves that we have earned it. It is when I turn my back to the light, and try to forget the origin of my being, that my best plans are discomfited, and my best wishes fail.

And, as God has made us, and being what we are, what we want is, to go and come in the light, to claim its benefit always, and to be using it every day. The man who expects to return to his Saviour truly, on any season of communion, on any festival of the Church, or on the recurrence of Sunday here, must carry with him, Monday, Tuesday, and Wednesday, a Saviour's message, and the spirit of a Saviour's life. I cannot spend Saturday night in a gambler's hell, and come out sleek and clean, with changed clothes and a new heart, to the enjoyment of Sunday's worship. I cannot, through the week, domineer over my household like a tyrant, assert myself and my own luxury as the centre of the thought of a whole family, and then on Sunday sit decorous here, or elsewhere saying, "Lord have mercy upon us miserable offenders!" with any real hope that worship, hymn, or sermon are to help me largely. The disciples who took comfort in a Saviour when they returned were those who had engaged in a Master's business upon their journey.

From Thanksgiving to Fast.

FIFTEEN SERMONS

BY

EDWARD E. HALE.

THE GREAT HARVEST YEAR,
LOOKING BACK,
RITUAL,
PRAYER,
RESPECTABILITY,
YOURSELVES
WHAT IT IS TO BE CATHOLIC,
THE JOY OF LIFE,
THE ASSOCIATED CHARITIES,
THE REVISION OF THE BIBLE,
THE BIBLE,
LENT,
NEW LIFE,
BLASPHEMY AGAINST THE HOLY GHOST,
THE FUTURE OF NEW ENGLAND.

Price in paper covers, $1.00; in cloth binding, $1.25.

A second series (of fifteen) of Mr. Hale's sermons is now being issued, of which there have already been printed

THE LIFE IN COMMON,
BODY, MIND, AND SOUL,
BODILY TRAINING,
MENTAL DISCIPLINE,
CANDOR IN THE PULPIT,
SPIRITUAL EXERCISES,
DAILY BREAD,
HAPPY HOMES,
THE SEVENTY RETURNED.

Price, 10 cents per copy, or $1.00 for the series. Published by GEO. H. ELLIS, 101 Milk Street, Boston.

THE LATER PHARISEES.

A SERMON

PREACHED AT THE SOUTH CONGREGATIONAL CHURCH,

BOSTON, NOV. 16, 1879,

BY

EDWARD E. HALE.

BOSTON:

GEORGE H. ELLIS, 101 MILK STREET.

1879.

PRESS OF GEO. H. ELLIS, 101 MILK STREET.

THE LATER PHARISEES.

Woe unto you, Scribes and Pharisees.— MATTHEW xxiii., 15.

The more courageous critics for the last ten years have been saying kind things of the Pharisees. For eighteen hundred years, for reasons easily apprehended, they had been roughly mauled by Christian writers. There was an easy habit, when a preacher was too timid to blame the vices around him, for him to point his arrows at the old Pharisees, and to send the bolt home. Now a reaction — not to be wondered at — has given a check to this attack. The last twenty years have given wholly new attention to those four centuries, once so blank and so mysterious, between the Old Testament and the New ; and as those centuries of the history of Israel have been worked out, it appears that the Pharisees were originally the national party, who preserved the purity of the nation's life as against all trimmers, who consorted with Greeks or other outlandish rulers. It is with such reasons that we hear bold and conscientious speakers, now, alluding to those "brave and determined Pharisees," those "patriotic Pharisees," those "Pharisees who were the Puritans of Israel," claiming for them indeed the same respect which the intelligence of our time now generally claims for the Puritans of England and of New England, two hundred years ago.

All the same the truth remains that the Saviour, with hardly an exception, speaks of them with disapproval, almost amounting to contempt. And in the very crisis of his fate, as if from a sense of duty, that he might leave no question as to what he thought them, he pronounces this woe upon them. We can tone it down. And there is an anecdote of Dr. Channing which describes him as reading the woe so that the wrath it shows was indeed the "wrath of the Lamb." Still, tone it down as we may, it stands as a most distinct avowal of Christ's righteous indignation. If he knew his own time, and the men of his own time, the Pharisees of his

4

own time deserved very nearly the verdict which, on the whole, history has pronounced upon them.

Nor is it difficult to discover the basis of both these estimates of this body of partisans. Partisans they were, as their very name implies. Pharisees means men who set themselves apart, or as we now say, " Separatists " or " Sectarians." All history is full of instances where the name of a party survives the organization which first took the name, and the objects for which the organization was formed. And that man would make a sad botch, who, having acquainted himself with the policy of the " Whigs," who took that name in New England before the revolution, should try by what he knew of them to explain the canvass of the whigs who voted for Henry Clay. So there is no thread of connection, however slight, which pretends to unite the republican party of Jefferson with the republican party of to-day. Under different circumstances, these parties came into being, and the identity of name is a mere accident. Differences as wide as this separate the patriotic Pharisee party of the time of Judas Maccabæus from the Pharisee hair-splitters of the time of Jesus Christ.

I think that that steady degradation of theirs, fine by degrees and miserably less, is worth our study by way of caution. It will point out the dangers which attend what is called " culture," and which have, in fact, with us made the word " culture " contemptible. Nay, it will prove more : it will prove that the moment a class separates itself from other classes, in that moment this process begins by which it cares for small things instead of great things, and, in its eagerness for extreme polish, neglects substance and quality.

This is precisely the history of the decline of the Pharisees, from the days of their patriotism to what we call the days of Pharisaism. You may illustrate the same thing in the decline of the Roman nobility. They were once the men who in their hardihood compelled a world to obey them. They come out in the lower empire, the most degraded sensualists that the world has ever known. Or take the decline in the English kings, from Alfred, who fought at the head of his army, slept on the ground, if need were, and offered his life, if need were,— from William the Conqueror, or from Richard the Lion-hearted, who did the same thing. Take the decline till you come down to Charles I., bred in the purple, or to Charles II., or, by another leap of a century, to George the Prince Regent, afterwards George IV.

Richard the Lion-hearted may have been as luxurious, when it was time for luxury, as any of them. Still, he could sleep in a bivouac, he could risk his life, he could cut down a Saracen with his battle-axe. He could direct his army. He could have said what Henry IV. said, "Rally round my white plume!" When you come down to poor Charles I., you have a brave man indeed,— a man not unwilling to die, nor unfit to die, but a man wholly unable to lead. He has to do the business of governing by proxy; by the hand of Laud or Wentworth or Rupert, he does what a leader ought to do. Come down to Charles II., and you have scarcely a figure-head. The best he can do is to play croquet in Pall Mall. And when, a hundred years after, you have come down to George, afterward George IV., he cannot even play croquet. He can play dice and cards, and can come to Parliament, to ask them to pay his gambling debts. History is all full of such degeneracy, where a particular class is kept separate from other classes, is not recruited by the best blood there is, or does not live by Paul's great law,— that God has made of one blood all men in all the world.

Of this decline, the law seems always to be the same. Your separated class, your Pharisee, makes clean the outside of the cup and the platter. That is Jesus' phrase, and it serves perfectly all along. He is superficial. He is interested in accomplishments more than in substance. If he study language, he is worried about pronunciation and delicacies of accent to an extent that makes him forget the literature, and its aim and compass. If he study music, he is devoted to marvels of execution, instead of attempting to interpret the profound mysteries of the great masters. If he go into society, his thought is on the finesse of deportment, and does not grapple with the realities of conversation. Dress in his life becomes merely an opportunity of external decoration. Art is nothing more; and under the sway of such people you will find false ornament in architecture pasted upon the outside of walls, instead of the dignity of severe work, in which nothing comes in but it serves a purpose. It would not be difficult to trace the law of personal degradation by which the Pharisee or separatist, in proportion as he has come to think that God has not made him as other men are, turns his chief attention in such ways, to the outside. He is superficial, and he lets the substance go.

The first exhibition of this superficiality appears in criticism. Criticism ought to be the judgment carefully passed, for good or for ill, upon whatever work has been done,— so passed that the workman himself can work better another time, so passed that he shall be encouraged for what he has done well, while at the same time he is warned if he have been careless. But in a superficial age, or in a circle of Pharisees, criticism becomes simply fault-finding; and I am sorry to say, that such is the popular and careless use of the word with us to-day. You shall see a newspaper writer, after praising what pleases him, say, " It is now time to criticise ; " as if criticism were necessarily blame. Now the first requisite for a judge or critic — the two words here mean the same thing — is, that he put himself into the place of the workman whose achievement he considers. To put myself in his place, I must sympathize. I must comprehend the object, enter heartily into the effort for it, and make the workman's cause my own. He must not feel that I am looking down superior from above. He must understand that his wish and mine are the same. I shall show him what is wrong; yes, but I shall also show him what is right, and shall show my pleasure that it is right. In one of the first interviews I ever had with our great artist, Mr. William Hunt, he dwelt most eagerly on the merit of the drawing of a child of six years old, whom I had never seen and did not know : " Nothing right in it, of course, as these fellows count right," he said. " Of course the child could neither make a straight line nor a crooked one,— but then there was so much *go* to it. She expressed what she meant to express. The action and fire were there." The story expresses precisely his sympathy with everybody who was really trying to do anything well,— whether it were in the world of art, where he was master pre-eminent, or in any other world; for his sympathy was as certain for one sphere as for another. It was that sympathy which made all his criticism invaluable, and gave such worth to all his instructions. Compare that against the niggling dissections of the self-called critic, whose first object is to show how much he knows himself; and whose second object is to show how little any one else knows. The picture has all been painted for us, in the sketch of these Pharisees, who pile heavy burdens and grievous to be borne,— who shut up the kingdom of heaven against men. It is of this class of critics, self-styled such, that Mr. D'Israeli says very fairly, that critics are persons, who, having failed in literature themselves, are appointed judges of those who have succeeded. Of such criticism as theirs, the characteristic is invariably its neglect of the substance and its attention to the outside.

It was my duty, once, for many years, to examine what are called the literary criticisms passed by the journals of this country upon the new books. From the work of three hundred critics, I might except that of ten as being first fairly addressed to the substance of the thing done or attempted, and afterward to the method or outside. For the rest, the pattern was almost invariable. The writer either said of the poem, or the novel, or the speech: "This is just like what this man has said before. Why does he keep saying the same thing in the same way always?" Or he said: "This is entirely unlike what this man has ever said before. Why does he not hold to the safe old ground, where he has won his victories?" And in general the so-called critic was eager to show that he should have written himself the book, which in fact had been written by another. So rare is the divine sympathy by which one man shares another's work, interests himself in another's purpose, descends to a knowledge of another's difficulties, and fairly tries to bear another's burdens.

The decline from the patriotism of the Pharisee, whom Judas Maccabæus called to defend his country, down to the petty conceit of the Pharisee whom our Saviour describes, is the same change as that which gives two meanings to the word Puritan. The Puritan who charged with Cromwell at Marston Moor, the Puritan who wrote Paradise Lost and Lycidas, the Puritan who crossed the ocean and made New England was a man of purity, as his name imports, and of courage and conduct, as is testified by the establishment of a great commonwealth in each hemisphere. He was, as well, sympathetic, tender, kind, true, and gentle; or we should not count among puritans such names as Milton and Marvell, Winthrop and Winslow. But when you come two generations later, you find the Puritan exhibited in Cotton Mather straining at a gnat and swallowing a camel — counting up jots and tittles in the letter of the law, careful for the outside, and leaving what was within ghastly and foul. Nor do I say all of that decline, if I stop here. Outside of this State, there is the impression that in our own city there lingers the pettiness of the puritan's precision. Men say of people who were born in Boston, as I was, for instance, and have grown up here, as I have, that we are interested in petty things, and do not compass the great realities; that we are elegant even to finesse in the love of external culture; but that we neglect weightier matters of the true law, in our eagerness for these superficial trifles. All this charge must make us watchful. We must not let Boston decline from the Boston which made the Revolution,—from which the true democracy started, as Mr. Carlyle says, on its march around the world. Boston must always be the Boston which, to the modern world first unfolded the plan of the education of all the people by the people. Boston must always be the Boston which Boston was in 1780, when the first complete written Constitution which ever rested on the vote of the people here went into operation. Boston must always be the Boston which gave to Channing his home; and was not satisfied to maintain for herself, but proclaimed broadcast to mankind the gospel in which every man is the well-beloved child of God, and may come to his throne without fear and without price. Grant these substantials — so many heritages from the real Puritanism of our fathers — and the rest will take care of itself. Cleanse first the inside of the cup and the platter, and the outside will be clean also.

Life, and more life, life, and larger life, make Christ's purpose so completely that he and his look with little patience on these short-hand methods which would secure deportment by practising deportment; would secure fine art by the practice of technicalities, or in any way secure accomplishments without care for vital power. As well secure leaves when there is no root to the tree, or flowers on a sandbeach where there is nothing to feed the plant. The master of ceremonies tries it when his sovereign enters the city in triumph. He covers with green branches this pile of dirt or that ruined wall; and, for the honor of the pageant, the leaves are fresh and bright: but the next day they are curling up under the sun; the next, they are brown and dry, and he must remove them quickly, or they will be more corrupt than the deformities they cover. Of the whole Christian gospel, this demand for life within is central; and here is the reason why that gospel is so indifferent to any description of method,—even of the organization of its church,—quite silent about ritual or form. Only be sure that life lives and grows within. Care for the heart from which come the issues of life, and for the rest these genuflexions and prostrations, these washings of hands and immersions, this incense and bell-ringing may all go. Let life drink from the fountain of life; let the spirit be alive with the Holy Spirit, quick and true, and there is no fear but method, accomplishment, and technicality shall follow in decorous and convenient order.

In education, in politics, nay, in business life, to be caring only for details,— nervous and fussy about the dotting of an i, or the crossing of a t, while one forgets the supreme object of education, the supreme object of politics, the supreme object in business,— this is the sign of the perverted Pharisee,— the Pharisee whom the Saviour ridicules in his early life, against whom he pronounces woe before he dies. In education, to be piling in this new science, and that last finesse; to forget that our whole object is to teach the pupil how to learn, and that we degrade education when we merely make the child commit to memory a string of recipes for life. In politics, to be finding fault with this blunder, to be paring off this expenditure, to be investigating that fraud,— instead of spending the main strength in purifying the heart of the State, raising to the highest the motives of the voter, and in whatever way giving more life to the body of which he is one member. So, in business, it is poor Phariseeism which supposes that by this trick of publicity,— as a man might pray at the corners of the street,— by that spasm of parsimony, as a man might tithe mint and anise and cumin, — he is going to carry out the central object of business life. This is to smooth the hard work of living by bringing producer and consumer nearer, by helping man to serve man, and really knitting closer together the parted world. So it is in religion, which is the life of education, of politics, and of business. It is only a Pharisee in the decline of Phariseeism who will distress himself about this Shibboleth, or that Sibboleth, which his convert must pronounce. It is only such a Pharisee who will be anxious about this rite or that rite, more water or less water, this jot or that tittle. It is only such a Pharisee who will care for this costume or that costume. Let life make the forms of life. Let life find its own costume. Let life work its own victory. Let life find its own expression. No fear for that if life lives and grows. No fear, if you love the Lord your God with your whole heart and strength and mind and soul.

From Thanksgiving to Fast.

FIFTEEN SERMONS

BY

EDWARD E. HALE.

THE GREAT HARVEST YEAR,
LOOKING BACK,
RITUAL,
PRAYER,
RESPECTABILITY,
YOURSELVES
WHAT IT IS TO BE CATHOLIC,
THE JOY OF LIFE,
THE ASSOCIATED CHARITIES,
THE REVISION OF THE BIBLE,
THE BIBLE,
LENT,
NEW LIFE,
BLASPHEMY AGAINST THE HOLY GHOST,
THE FUTURE OF NEW ENGLAND.

Price in paper covers, $1.00; in cloth binding, $1.25.

A second series (of fifteen) of Mr. Hale's sermons is now being issued, of which there have already been printed

THE LIFE IN COMMON,
BODY, MIND, AND SOUL,
BODILY TRAINING,
MENTAL DISCIPLINE,
CANDOR IN THE PULPIT,
SPIRITUAL EXERCISES,
DAILY BREAD,
HAPPY HOMES,
THE SEVENTY RETURNED,
THE LATER PHARISEES,
EMIGRATION TO KANSAS.
BREAD ALONE.

Price, 10 cents per copy, or $1.00 for the series. Published by GEO. H. ELLIS, 101 Milk Street, Boston.

BREAD ALONE.

Man doth not live by bread only.—DEUT. viii., 3.

I was obliged, on Thanksgiving day, to be satisfied with a single word of warning, in which I might repeat the eternal lesson of this text. In the midst of the unmatched bounty of God, of granaries overflowing with food, of a harvest, of which no small part perishes where it grows, because the market is so distant, the need of this warning comes; for the danger always comes in. Men think they can live by bread alone, and they are determined to try. With plenty, there comes conceit, and, with conceit, impiety. That lesson has been taught the world, if the world were only more apt at learning, many, many times; and the prophet of the time, whoever he may be, has to speak the most eagerly in the moments of highest prosperity. As Israel marches into the Promised Land, the days of famine ended, and the milk and honey within their grasp, Moses has to remind them of the varied care by which God has led them, " That he might teach you to know that man does not live by bread alone, but by every word that cometh from the mouth of God." And when, centuries after, Jesus Christ meets the temptations with which his infinite work begins, he recurs to the same lesson, and gives to it even a wider significance. He spurns that temptation at which so many men stumble! Whatever his gifts are, he will not use them for bread for himself,— not he! " Man shall not live by bread alone, but by every word that cometh from the mouth of God."

What is God's word, then? Certainly more than any particular oracle in any particular book.

What is God's word, for any nation, in any time? This is a question for any nation. What else does he give it besides bread for men to eat? What other laws must a man follow, or a nation follow, besides these laws of spring-time and harvest, which go to the make-up of national wealth? The school of the political economists, dating from Adam Smith, whose great book is a twin with the Declaration of Independ-

4

ence, published in 1776,— this school has, for a hundred
years, tried to persuade us, that for nations, at least, Moses
was wrong in this matter, and Jesus Christ was wrong. The
doctrine of the political economists is, that nations as
nations, and their rulers as rulers, are simply to study
the physical side of things. Let the nation grow rich, they
say, and everything else will follow, if, indeed, there be
anything else to follow,— the most corn possible, the most
cotton possible, the most iron possible, and the most machinery : with these victories, you have done all that government
must try to do. Let the rest go.

To which proclamation, repeated never so craftily, the
reply of each Testament, the reply of every prophet, the
reply of history, is the reply of the heart of man.

"Man shall not live by bread alone " : God has other
words, and many of them : man must live by those. There is
the word of mutual love : man must live by that. There is
the word of beauty : man must live by that. There is the
hope of heaven : man must live by that. There is the word
of right: man must live by that. Not by bread only, which
feeds his body, but by every word that feeds his mind, and
by every word that feeds his heart, must man live."

"Is not all that poetry?" asks Mr. Gradgrind. "I hate
poetry."

Dear Mr. Gradgrind, it is poetry. And we know that you
hate poetry ; we know that you are never so happy as when
you are seated at a lonely board, with a raging appetite, with
a perfect dinner spread before you ; when no nonsense of
conversation,— of anxiety about to-morrow, or of duty for
to-day, intervenes ; nothing to prevent your own personal, and
selfish, physical enjoyment of that meal. We know that you
hate poetry, and that Adam Smith hated it, and that Mr.
Mill had not the very faintest conception of what the word
"poetry" meant. All the same, dear Mr. Gradgrind, we
mean that your children shall have pleasures which you cannot conceive ; and theirs shall have more. They shall live
lives which you cannot conceive, and their children shall
have life which abounds yet more : for God reigns, and man
is his child : and man shall not live by bread alone, but
by every word that proceedeth out of the mouth of God shall
man live.

It is, indeed, to the poets of every time and tribe — times

the darkest and tribes the most barbarous — that men owe
the steady protest which lifts them from feeding like beasts,
and teaches them the worth of an idea. Beasts live by their
food only, and for their food alone. To man it is given to
look above his food, even upon God and the infinite heaven.
The meanest medicine-man among the Sioux Indians has
come upon this truth, and enforces it. Milton, Dante,
Homer, in their own matchless way repeat it ; and such is the
subtle revenge of history and life, that though such princes as
these beg their way while they live ; though, in their day, the
corn-contractors, the bakers, the butlers, the cooks of the
" *cordon-bleu,*" and the men who direct matchless vintages, out-
bragged them, out-shone them, and despised them,— as time
passes, all these people who lived by bread alone, and for
bread alone, are forgotten. But cities contend for the honor
of being Homer's birthplace, " through which the living
Homer begged his bread "; and Florence grateful at last,
tries her very best in building Dante's monument.

Here comes in, for instance, the immortality of the Scriptures. Critics can make nothing of it. The men of science
stumble, and are provoked at it ; they cannot account for it.
The truth is, that, from the first chapter of Genesis, where
God spoke and there was light, the Word of God asserts
itself as the ruling power. That is the theme of the Bible,
till you come out at the end, on the last chapters of the book
of Revelation, where all power is given to him whose talisman is this same " Word of God." Why will a unanimous
world turn back to this old story,— older than Moses, older
than the Hebrews,— which begins : " God said, Let there be
light " ? Why does not the world accept, in preference, our
somewhat stupid statement, which says that in the beginning
something was ; and then another thing happened to come
out from the something ; and then from the other thing yet a
third thing evolved itself ? Why does the world cling to the
imagery of the first chapter of Genesis ? Because a man who
believed in Ideas first sang this song, and not a man who
believed in Things. An Idealist, who knew God, and loved
God, perhaps had seen God, knew that man could not live
by things alone, and said so. This poet — that is to say, this
man of an Idea — gave to the " Word of God " its fit place
in the business of creation. *God said,* " Let there be Light ! "
and Light was.

God said, " Let there be Land ! " and Land was.

God said, "Let there be food!" and the fruit-tree bore fruit.

And God looked on all that he had made ; and behold, it was very good!

And God made man like himself.

The Idealist, the poet, who put in words the beginning of the Bible, does not leave you or me to think we can live by things alone, by the bread that feeds our hunger least of all.

But by every word that proceedeth out of the mouth of God doth man live.

And so you pass through the Bible. There are dreary genealogies in it. Yes. There are old rituals,— out-grown to-day, even inexplicable. Yes. There are the outbreaks of prophets against kings and rulers, of whom we know nothing. Yes. There are proverbs of very questionable morality. Yes. But in it all, even behind the *chevaux de frise* of the most antiquated and worthless annals or documents, there is this same reverence for the Idea as greater than the Thing. The Word of God is master ; and the mere fact obeys. All the rulers — Joshua, Gideon, Samuel, David, Judas Maccabæus — conquer when they are obedient to an idea, when they obey the Word of God ; and, when they refuse allegiance to it, they fail.

So the book rolls on to its triumphat close. At the end of the inexplicable imagery, the wild, weird narrative of the book of Revelation, the story is still the triumph of the Word of God.

Inexplicable, if you please, the allegory. But the conclusion is clear as the light. Rivers of blood, flaming cities, plagues of wild beasts, armies of tyrants, every figure of anguish, torture, and death have been heaped together in the wildest fancy of the excited poet ; that with the more vivid contrast he may exhibit the steady progress and complete triumph of what God says shall be done,— of the Word of God. At that word also armies gather, as at the rallying cries of tyrants and conquerors. That Word also asserves its crown, by a right more sure than that of usurpers who strike for it in battle. That Word of God, which is the still small voice, when it is speaking to Elijah in the desert, which is gentle encouragement heard by Jesus in the Jordan, when none except him heard it, is here the Word of thunder which speaks as well to those who would fain harden their hearts, and close their ears : and to them it speaks, so that they know that here is the crowned monarch of the world. His name is King of kings and Lord of lords !

It is impossible to think that it is by mere accident that all this gorgeous imagery of triumph makes the end of the New Testament. The true end of all gospel, of all warning, and of all counsel comes when He reigns whose right it is to reign ; when the armies of those who listen to the Word of God and follow enter into their inheritance ; when the city of God comes down out of heaven, and when all tears are wiped from all eyes. This is the great *denouement* to the great drama which we call history. The seer, or prophet, or poet, whether caged in the Island of Patmos, or wherever, looking backward or forward, only differs from other men in that he sees a whole day's march, where they only see the dust around them ; or perhaps he sees the year's harvest, where they only see the furrow of to-day's labor ; or perhaps he sees the century of a nation's redemption, where they only see the girding for to-day's battle, or the nursing of the wounds of yesterday. The seer looks down the line of time, foreshortens the whole picture, and projects upon one canvass all the imagery of this century, and the next, and the next, so that you may see them all together. There is no confusion to him. The only confusion is to us, who, with but halting understanding, only indistinctly follow his song. The plagues and the victories, the vials of wrath and the pæans of rejoicing, are all described at once to us ; and we do not fitly discriminate, nor see how the one leads up to — nay, compels — the other.

Of the whole Bible history, I say this; I may say it of all. The central law, the movement of the plot, shall I say ? is the steady triumph of the Word of God, of the law of God, the wish and purpose of God. We say this and that is dramatic, when some great new piece of history is unfolded before our eyes. What do we mean ? We make a reference to the old law of the Greek drama, in which their hard and cruel destiny forced itself into human affairs, trampled down this affection, silenced that sob, and overawed that struggle ; and so, in defiance of men's wish and men's hopes, asserted the dumb, dead power of cruel fate. There is just a reference to that stern certainty. But the true drama of history to us means a different progress, under a law not blind, but full of light ; not cruel, but quick with love. It is the certain unveiling of the sun from the first cold gray of morning, through the pearl, and amber, and purple of dawn, to the glory of his arising. For it is the certain advance of the purpose of God, that sickness shall be healed and sins remitted and held back, and death itself be known as the nothing that it is. It is the visible display on the stage of human life, and, in the scenes of our common being, of the eternal purpose of God, in which sorrow and sighing shall be done away, and all tears shall be wiped from all eyes. Such is the great drama which we call history; and the man who is competent to show us that, by whatever symbolism, is the poet, the prophet, or the seer.

It is, indeed, as one age differs from another in its sense of this certain triumph of the Idea that we find one or another era to be alive or dead, interesting or dull, to read about. It is in proportion as one man differs from another man in following an Idea — the noblest Ideal that he can find or make — that he is worthy of our regard and enthusiasm. Take the history of the last century, from Queen Anne's time to the American Revolution, and, whatever may be the curiosity with which the novelist or museum collector may overhaul it, it is as dead as Ninevah, for any encouragement, any enthusiasm, any life, which the reader gains from its great people. They seem to have been, all their lives long, stepping right and left, backward and forward, in the measured paces of a minuet, with no wish nor object but to do what was set down for them to do, well-pleased, indeed, when by some good chance the performance were all done; and well they might be. While, on the other hand, you have only to take the period of the English Rebellion or of our own Revolution, when men had a great purpose under them, above them, before them, and around them; and because great and small, peasant and prince, all glow with one noble life, every word of history quickens you. You read with a purpose now, and for your own life you learn a lesson. That lesson is only one illustration more of the eternal lesson,— the lesson of the New Testament, as it is of all inspired scripture,— that the Word of God is more mighty than kings, more lordly than lords; that it goes forward armed with infinite power, and that, in the end, all the armies of the world must follow it.

As history and life were, when this seer of the Revelation wrote out his visions of the triumph of the Word, the deference to an Idea, and firm obedience to it on the part of man, though it led them to agony and death, had been most nobly, as most often illustrated in the Jewish race.

That wonderful list of martyrs, which I have read to you from the Epistle to the Hebrews, illustrates every word of the book of the Revelation. These are all men who live by the Idea,— by the evidence, as that writer says, of things not seen. They do not wait for the proofs that what they do will give them fine clothes or palaces, bread or butter, oil or wine : they live by the Idea ; they live by the Idea of right, the Idea of truth ; they obey, as this writer says, the Word of God. Other history was not without witness,— as when Pythias died for his friend,— as when Regulus died rather than break his word. But, on the whole, it would be fair to say, that in the days when this seer wrote, the men of Greece did what they liked, and that the men of Rome did what they were bidden ; while the men of Judea, and the new-born church which sprang from them, had given and were giving to the world the noblest instances of life for an Idea. Then comes in the cataclysm,— the great revolution,— which changes history, and lifts all life to a plane which is wholly new. There comes in this gospel, given first, and last, and always, to the statement that men must live for the Idea, and the agonizing prayer that they may. " Why are ye so faithless ? " and, " What would you not do if you had more faith ? " These are all so many pleas, or so many demands, for Ideal life ; that a man shall look upward to the highest, forward for the best, and live by the noblest that he knows. This is the gospel, whose written canon ends, not undesignedly, with this triumphal song of the Revelation, in which the Word of God is made the conqueror of all kings and all lords. And this gospel has made the history of eighteen hundred years, to be wrought out, and written out on a plane wholly different from any history before.

Thus in all Jewish history there never was any such instance of fidelity to a great Idea, as that by which Columbus revealed this half the world to the other. That was faith,— as purely religious faith, as all the testimonies show, as was the faith of the Maccabees ; and an instance,— of which the effects appear everywhere to-day,— filtrating into every artery of the circulation of the world ; an instance where the faith of one man, his fidelity to an Idea, subdued kingdoms, wrought righteousness, stopped the mouths of lions, waxed valiant in fight, is in the history of Luther,— where a peasant miner's son dictated the new law of history, because he also believed, and lived in his belief. For us here, an instance, of which we may see the monuments every day, without so much as leaving our homes, was in the resolution and the performance of the English Puritans. They had got hold of an Idea, or, if you choose, an Idea had got hold of them. They were possessed by it. They could not eat nor sleep nor wake but that it interposed and asserted itself,— first, last, always. That man was his own priest, that was the Idea ; that man could direct, and must direct, his own worship, his own communion with God. And the Archbishop of England chose to say that he would direct their worship. No! not he, though all the armies of England were behind him. There are deserts so distant that the armies of England cannot strike there. There are winters so cold that even his spies cannot abide them. To those winters and to those deserts we will go. And they came. And that deference to an Idea, from that moment, gives to the history of the States they founded, all that is noble, or worth man's long consideration. Like other States, those States have had their turns of material prosperity and material failures. They strike a mine of wealth in their fisheries, or they compass the world in their discoveries, or they renew and revolutionize commerce by their inventions. But these things are vulgar, as all things are. These things perish, as pyramids perish. These things are forgotten ; but when this Puritan race stands for an Idea,— lives for it, and dies for it,— then it writes, as in letters of gold upon a tablet of adamant, one variation more on the eternal theme, which was sounded first when this poet wrote of one who shall be King of kings and Lord of lords, whose name is the "Word of God."

When this Puritan race crossed the ocean, because their Idea led them into exile, there was one of these new symphonies on the eternal strain. When they determined that every man and woman, every boy and girl, should be educated with the same privilege as his brother most favored, there sounded another. When, with all their heart and soul, their prophets and martyrs attempted the conversion of the Indian races, there was another. When in their town meetings, the little hill towns of some twenty log-cutters, one by one, voted war against the British Empire, because the rights of men were imperilled, forsooth, there was another. And when within the memory of those of us who are older, this same brood of men took up the statement of St. Paul, that all men were of one blood, and chose to carry that statement out

to its ultimate,— to force it to its legitimate results, land them
where it might,— that new departure, in an old voyage, was
yet another.

If only that old Puritan frenzy could be revived a little,
and men determine to worship more for themselves, and less
by proxy! What is the man who takes his opinion as he
finds it in a leading article, buying four cents' worth of
opinion every morning, in the market, and using it that day
for his own, but the lineal descendant of the man who took
his creed as Archbishop Laud or Leo the X. told him to?
Little of the Puritan in that convenient abnegation of opinion !
And the man who selects such or such a church, because
"they " do not there worry him with questions of conscience,
because "they" have "entered into their rest," has quite
forgotten the Idea which made the country to which he is
born. "Why not of your own selves judge ye what is right ? "
That cutting question is addressed to us, as much as to the
Pharisees. It is the personal question, for every man of us,
to ask what is for him the word of God to-day. He is only
running backward, back to the brute's state, if deaf to that
word of God ; he is trying to live by bread alone.

And here is the lesson which I would fain connect with the
rejoicings for an unheard of harvest with which the year goes
by. Is this land of ours willing to die the death of Carthage
or of Tyre,— lands which were great in commerce, great in
riches, but not great in men ? Are our republics willing to
repeat the fate of the Italian republics, which exiled their
Dantes, even their Columbuses, their Cabots, and their Ves-
pucci, so that those heroes won their laurels under other
banners? If not, if we look forward to any greatness in our
forecast of the future, it is by rejecting the bribe to turn all
our stones into bread, and by looking for every Word of God,
by our loyalty to an Idea. What if some poor Indian tribe
stand in the way of our harvesting ? Right is right ; and the
nation must respect its own treaties with those red men.
What if there be a temptation here or there to sacrifice the
national Idea at the demand of an old world hierarchy ?
Right is right ; and the nation must show that it lives by every
Word of God,— that it is true to an Idea.

And, not to speak of the nation or its government, you and
I, who may think we have little share in such concerns, meet
just the same necessity in our separate lives. Did not the
Saviour meet it ? And how shall we escape ?

We are called — quite as certainly as ever he was called — to live by the Idea, the eternal Idea; to follow, and with white garments, too, this King of kings and Lord of lords, whose name is the *Word of God.* There is not an hour when some other sovereign does not try to enlist us. Not an hour when this bribe or that pretence — a shilling here, or a ribbon there, now a stone turned into bread, now the sway of some devil's kingdom — is not offered us. Yes, and all around us are those who will say we are fools if we refuse. All around us are those who will say we had best eat the bread, if it seems like bread, though it be made of desert sands. There are those who will tell us we had better take the bribe, if it be really gold, though it come from the devil's hand. But, all the same, the voice of all history echoes one and the same clarion cry. Even this history of the present hour, in all its dusᵗ and intrigue, is repeating it. The song of every poet sings it ; the death of every martyr proves it. It is the first word of Genesis ; it is the last word of the Revelation ; it is the proclamation of the whole Gospel,— that the wish of God, his order and his direction, sway and rule the world. This is King of kings and Lord of lords.

They who follow it, though in dust and blood, are they who conquer ; and they who scorn it fail, and fail forever.

Heart, Mind, Soul, and Strength.

A SERMON

PREACHED AT THE SOUTH CONGREGATIONAL CHURCH,
DEC. 7, 1879, AND THE FIRST INDEPENDENT CHURCH,
BALTIMORE, DEC. 14, 1879,

BY

EDWARD E. HALE.

BOSTON:

GEORGE H. ELLIS, 101 MILK STREET.

1879.

GEO. H. ELLIS, Printer, 101 Milk Street, Boston.

HEART, MIND, SOUL, AND STRENGTH.

Thou shalt love the Lord thy God with all thy heart, and with all
thy soul, and with all thy mind, and with all thy strength.— MARK ii., 30.

The statement is the best they could make of that union
of man with God, which we call by the much-abused name
of piety,— which perhaps in our time is better expressed by
the words " Devotion " or " Communion." These words are
not yet worn out, as, alas ! the great word " Piety " begins
to be.

It is a sad thing to confess, but it is true, that the statement which is meant to be all tenderness and sympathy is,
in truth, one of the stumbling-blocks of the faith of sensitive people. So hard is it to make language do its duty. In
the confidence given to a minister, I have had people, I dare
not say how many, come to me to confess that they do not
love God. " I can serve him, I can thank him, I can praise
him, but I do not love him. I do not love him as I love my
sister, my mother, my brother, or my child." Such is the
confession which I have received more than a hundred times
from sensitive people, brave enough to tell the truth, wise
enough to analyze the course of their own lives, and too
proud to assume a virtue which they do not have.

I have always counted it as very fortunate that, in answer
to such sensitive and brave people, one has ready the text
which St. John happened to let fall, writing with quite another object, " If one love not his brother, whom he hath
seen, how can he love God, whom he hath not seen ? " When
people have been hurt by a text, another text is always the
better remedy for the wound. For, if your patient is in that
unhappy mood of mind which Paul calls word-worshipping,
you must generally, at the start, take him as you find him.
You must, at the start, administer your medicine as you can ;
hoping that this symptom, also, will die out with the rest of
the disease. If St. John chose to admit that our love of an

unseen Infinite Being differed in its quality or in its method
from the love we bear to those close around us, we need not
try to go beyond him, the loving apostle. Let us recognize, from the beginning, the truth that finite beings, like ourselves, do not comprehend the Infinite as we do each other.
And let us, while we use the best language we can, admit,
all the time, that language is limited. It is at best but a
thing, or a series of things. We will do the best we can with
it. Doing this, Moses, as he wrote the Law, used this word,
which, in the different languages, we have translated by the
great word Love, the best we have. Love expresses the
closest connection possible of confidence and help between
two lives. And when Moses says, "Love God," he says,
"Come to him as closely as you can; unite his life with
your life as closely as you know how." When Jesus cites
and approves the direction, he says the same thing; and in
a thousand ways, all through his life, he so illustrates what he
means as to show that he does not command the impossible.·
That is not his way.

You love the baby in your arms with the eagerness of a
mother. You can, and you will, supply what his ignorance
makes necessary. You can, and you will, shield him where
his weakness demands. It would be simply absurd to pretend that your love of God could show itself in any such
methods or expressions. Or you love your newly married
wife with the eagerness of mutual respect, each day enlarging; and of the daily surprise, as you better and better understand each other. Here is the fulness of joy which comes
when two half lives — broken till now — fit each into the
other, and become one rounded whole. But, again, it would
be simply absurd to pretend that your love of God could
show itself in any such methods or expressions as those which
you two find natural, in that new-born life in union. Frankly
take this for granted, just as you take it for granted that
God, who is a spirit, has neither fingers nor hands, neither
feet nor arms. When Jesus asks you to love God, and
when he tells you that the command is one of the two great
commands of all, he means that you shall open your life to
God as fully as you can, and that from the life of God you shall
draw all you can draw. As in all duty, your responsibility
ends where your ability ends. You are not bidden to do
more than you can do. Bring God your best, and you will
bring the perfect offering.

5

I. In the exuberance of the Hebrew language, to express this best offering as well as they could, Moses piles up words of similar meaning after the injunction, to show that the whole spiritual nature of man is concerned in this intercourse with the Great Spirit of all. "Love God," he says, "with all your mind, and soul, and strength." Our rendering is not inadequate; and the vagueness necessary in such expression is found in the original language as much as it is in ours. "Give him your whole life," Moses says, "just as far and as fully as you can." The writers of the Gospels put into the mouth of the Jewish scribe and of Jesus corresponding words, though, as it happens, they do not use the same words, even as their own version produced them. And Mark and Luke go a little farther, and, to increase, if possible, the stringency and urgency of the whole, add another word; so that the requisition is that we love God with all our "heart, and soul, and mind, and strength." This is just as we should say,—we are to consecrate every spiritual power of our being.

II. Even were we textualists,—as, thank God, we are not,—there is no reason for pressing the four leading words of the text so as to contrast or define their shades of meaning. Neither Moses, nor the scribe, nor the Saviour had any such precision in their use of them; nor, if they had, are the shades the same in Hebrew as in Greek, nor in Greek as in English. What is demanded is the whole inner life of the man, and these words are chosen, as being all the words they had to express it; as a lawyer to-day takes all the words of a class and uses them together, when he wants to be sure that he carries the whole charge possible. But it does happen that the four English words have gained certain meanings, largely from the use which the New Testament makes of them; which serve us very closely in describing the dangers which come to the religious life, when a man lives it only partially, and does not give to it his whole being. Taking language as we use it to-day, a man's religion is twisted and one-sided, if he love God only with his heart; or, again, if he love him only with his mind; or, again, if he love him only with his soul; or if he do not love him with all his might. The risk of such one-sidedness was before the scribe, and it was before Jesus too. And the warning has been renewed in a thousand excesses of a thousand fanatics, from that day to this day.

III. Thus, let a man say that he loves God with all his heart; or let him say—what to a Trinitarian is the sar thing—that he loves Jesus with all his heart; and then let him add,—as half the rhapsodists do add,—consciously or not, that all the rest may go! Let him say, as I have heard revivalists say, that he cares nothing for intellectual religion or for rational religion,—the religion of the mind. Let him say that of himself he has no power and no might; that he cannot love God with all his strength, because he has none, and this is said very often. Let him say that heart-worship is all in all,—the heart's own love; but that what men call "aspiration"—the soaring of the human soul to the Infinite—is all transcendental fancy. And this is said thousands of times by people eager in their self-abasement. Such a man really says that he will love God with all his heart, while he does not love him with all his strength, with all his mind, and all his soul. And what such a man offers you, and what he enjoys, is simply what I am apt to call a "sugar-candy religion." I do not like to call it a religion of sentiment; for the word "sentiment" ought not to be flung away. It has caught in conversation the name of the religion of "gush." It is the religion of "religiosity"; and it earns that new-coined name, because it abandons reason, faith, and vigor.

Of which it is my duty to say the more, because in that passion for show and advertisement, which now appears everywhere, the teachers of religion have been specially tempted in our time to run into the extravagances which win, not unjustly, the bad names I have been citing. To assemble a large audience is the fair desire of every man who has to speak. And, alas! in the deficiency of true criticism in our time, a convenient way to judge of the truth of what a man says is to count the number of the people who listen. It is a convenient way, but a very bad way: It is, however, to the union of these two different causes that we owe the tendency to making the preaching of religion much more a matter of personal appeal, of what people call "personal magnetism." This results in making it a matter of the heart, as men say, more than of the soul of man, or of the reason of man, or of the strength of man. But the religion so fostered does not stand the test. There is but one test. "By their fruits shall ye know them." And when tried by that test, a merely emotional religion, born of rhetoric or of "personal magnetism," a human sympathy only, infallibly gives way.

This spongy or unreliable softness is no peculiarity of one

class of believers. It is a madness which now seizes on one
communion of Christians, then on another. Just now it is a
characteristic of those American churches which are ridding
themselves, as fast as they can, of old Calvinistic trammels.
It is now their habit to say that theirs is a religion of the
heart rather than of the head : as if the Saviour had not
warned us all against any religion which was not of both
together. The reaction is the more curious and instructive,
because in old Calvinism, which made these churches, as
indeed it made New England, they loved the Lord their God
with all their mind, and did not love him with the heart at
all. The condition was exactly counter to the error of to-
day. Whatever else we may say against Calvinism, we have
to confess that it was logical,— pitilessly logical. It took
its premises, and then followed its reasoning right through
without faltering, Puritan fashion. "But you destroy God's
character for mercy," pleaded the poor Arminians. "We
can't help that," said the Calvinist. "We must reason out
the plan, and go where the plan takes us." He was willing
to love God "with all his mind," — yes, and with all the
strength of logic, — but the rest must go. Go it did ! Any
heart-love of God, anything which differed from what the
Hebrews called the "fear of God," was unknown in that
logic-bred religion.

In quite another quarter, the reverence for mere intellectual
process in religion showed itself half a century ago or more in
New England. The peculiarity of the early Unitarian movement, so one-sided that it would be amusing were it not so
serious, was the serene conviction that men were to be saved
by mental training. It was then and there that the passion
for "culture" came in, which is wearing out by its own absurdity. Why, sensible people really seemed to think that
when they had made the right statement of duty, and had
made people learn it and understand it, they would all do
right simply because they knew how ! It seemed to be supposed that if you could only make all the convicts in the
State Prison commit the third part of the Geneva catechism
to memory, and understand it thoroughly, they would come
out from prison saints, and eager to live the life of saints
here and hereafter. Religion, the largest word of all, was
thus tied down to an act of the understanding only, as completely as it had been by those Calvinists whose excuses these
men deplored.

IV. To make a religion, again, which shall be all *soul*, has been the hope and effort of many a true man. Indeed, if we knew what the highest orders of archangels were, we might find that such a religion is theirs. But for men, who do have passions and affections, who do use minds to reason, and also who have to work with all their might, it does not answer. Still, to love God with all one's soul, and in no other way, as we now use those words, really describes very well the attitude of the mystic who is nothing but a mystic. Accurate language calls such a man a "quietist." I hope I need not say that I think all true religion begins in man's native appreciation of God, and of his own relationship with God. It means a great deal that a child, as soon as he knows anything, takes it for granted that he can control the stream, the wind, the wave ; that he can master the horse and the dog and the sheep. The child feels from the beginning that he is master, and not slave. He knows, when he comes to consider, that he is ally of the power which rules the world. Thus it is as one grows to know more and more that one is God's child. Thus it is that one's soul testifies to God and his power. To this native testimony of the soul, Jesus Christ always appeals. It is what he calls "faith," and a great pity it is that our faltering language gives no better word to express what he meant and said. So it happens that many a follower of his, knowing that the pure in heart see God, and that those who listen hear him, has loyally tried to construct all religion out of the soul's own intimations of its infinity and immortality. Such men are the quietists or pure mystics, as I said. Such an attempt is, in substance, the attempt of the more mystic Quakers. Such a religion has been expounded once and again by the pure Transcendentalists of our day. Their appeal to the " pure reason," when in that appeal they find the whole of life, may be fairly enough called loving God with all the soul, and attempting no other love. I owe those men too much — we all owe those men too much — not to thank them for every word they have spoken.

Without such rest in God there is no Christianity. Christianity is wholly based on such absolute recognition of the real presence of God now and here. But, all the same, Christianity is a religion of real love, and bids me love God with all my heart ; it is a religion of intelligence, and bids me love him with all my mind ; it is a religion of activity, and 's me love him with all my strength. I must seek for these loves while I cling to the other, and devote myself to him with all the inborn aspirations of my soul.

Yes: I must love him with all my strength. I think some of you will remember a very striking sermon which Mr. Dall once preached here, about those East Indians among whom he has spent so much of his active and useful life. He preached from this text. He pointed out the intellectual acumen of the Brahmin; he pointed out that indolent affectionateness which is central in the Indian character; he described, almost with humor, the readiness of the Eastern religionist to be absorbed in the Divinity he worships. Such men love their God, he said, with all their heart,— yes; with all their mind,—yes; with all their soul,— oh, yes! But with all their strength? oh, no!

As he considered the religions of the East,— from which as we know all our civilization began, and all our religion,— their failure comes from their giving no strength, no vigor, no energy to their religious conviction. Sentiment without power! Logic without power! Faith without power!

And you and I need not go to the East Indies to find such men or such belief. We need not go any day very far from home, to find men and women who give all their strength to matters which have no concern with God, or man's intercourse with God. A man may have thought out a very reasonable faith; or he may have plunged into the full vortex of an emotional religion; or he may be willing, after a fashion, to give his soul — if he chooses to own he has a soul — to God, and his worship; but he shall give all his strength to politics, to trade, to making stocks rise or fall, to building houses and selling them. How many men you see, who seem to have finished up the business of religion, once for all, in some season of excitement, and then to have forgotten all about it; as you see husbands and wives who seem to have exhausted tenderness and romance in the honeymoon after marriage, and thereafter to be indifferent to each other! How many men you see, who, having made decorous provision for the recognition of religion,— having taken a pew for the family, having bought a Bible for the side-table, having seen that the children are in a good Sunday-school,— give all their strength to other enterprises,— worshipping by proxy, reading the Bible by proxy, and teaching the children about God and heaven by proxy! All this subdivision of duty, this applying what the economists call the division of labor even to the interests of religion, traverses the first great commandment: we must love God with all our strength, and in no spasmodic nor half-way homage.

The love of a child for his father, growing, as I will not hesitate to say, to become more and more like the love of friend to friend; the love which says in perplexity, "I will tell him all about it: I will ask him what he thinks of it"; the love which does not wait for a set day before it writes a letter, but is glad at any moment to turn round,— if it is only to smile, to nod, to catch a glimpse of a friend so near. There is such a reality, and those next God have known it absolutely, as the sense of profound rest; the certainty of success, which comes to him who, in his daily walk, walks with God; who, when he is alone, questions God; who, with his last waking thought, reminds himself that he is sleeping in God's arms; whose first word, as he wakes in the morning, is like Adam's, in Milton's poem, the glad expression of thanks,—" How good it is that you are here!"

Of such intimacy, the Saviour gives the perfect example. He loved with all his heart, with all his soul, with all his mind,— yes, and with all his strength. This singles him out, and makes him Saviour, not of one life, but of a world.

With all his heart. "Father, I thank thee that thou hast heard me!"

With all his mind. So simple, so rational his instructions, that superstition and bigotry despair of the Gospels, as they make up their systems, and have to turn from Him to the blinder counsels of his interpreters.

With all his soul. To this hour he is prince of the idealists. Mysticism — in the simple sense of that word, man's absolute intercourse with God — has existed to no purpose except under the wing of Christianity.

And all this success of his is clearly because he loves his God with all his strength. To God's work in the world he gives every power of his life. So a startled world has been willing to grant the impossible, and to say he is God. He is no fanciful and tender dreamer, though fanciful and tender dreamers make him so; he is no sickly sentimentalist, though sickly sentimentalists make him so; he is no angular rationalist, though angular rationalists make him so. He is Saviour of the world, because he devotes every power

to God's purpose in saving it. There is no leader of men
who has shown such vigor,— vigor, pertinacity, and purpose.
John Baptist himself knew no more than Christ of deserts
and hunger. The whole of history, outside his history, shows
no plan of missions so comprehensive and successful as his.
Nor do all the martyrdoms do more than imitate the loyalty
and serenity of his martyrdom. This is the life and this the
victory of the Son of God, well beloved, who gives his whole
strength to his love of God.

In God he lives, in God he moves, in God he has his
being.

From Thanksgiving to Fast.

FIFTEEN SERMONS

BY

EDWARD E. HALE.

THE GREAT HARVEST YEAR,
LOOKING BACK,
RITUAL,
PRAYER,
RESPECTABILITY,
YOURSELVES
WHAT IT IS TO BE CATHOLIC,
THE JOY OF LIFE,
THE ASSOCIATED CHARITIES,
THE REVISION OF THE BIBLE,
THE BIBLE,
LENT,
NEW LIFE,
BLASPHEMY AGAINST THE HOLY GHOST,
THE FUTURE OF NEW ENGLAND.

Price in paper covers, $1.00; in cloth binding, $1.25.

A second series (of fifteen) of Mr. Hale's sermons is now being issued, of which there have already been printed

THE LIFE IN COMMON,
BODY, MIND, AND SOUL,
BODILY TRAINING,
MENTAL DISCIPLINE,
CANDOR IN THE PULPIT,
SPIRITUAL EXERCISES,
DAILY BREAD,
HAPPY HOMES,
THE SEVENTY RETURNED,
THE LATER PHARISEES,
EMIGRATION TO KANSAS,
BREAD ALONE,
THANKSGIVING,
HEART, MIND, SOUL, AND STRENGTH.

Price, 10 cents per copy, or $1.00 for the series. Published by GEO. H. ELLIS, 101 Milk Street, Boston.

THE PATTERN IN THE MOUNT.

A SERMON

PREACHED AT THE SOUTH CONGREGATIONAL CHURCH,
UNION PARK STREET, DEC. 21, 1879,

BY

EDWARD E. HALE.

BOSTON:

GEORGE H. ELLIS, 101 MILK STREET.

1879.

Geo. H. Ellis, Printer, 101 Milk Street, Boston.

THE PATTERN IN THE MOUNT.

"Look that thou make them after the pattern, which was shewed thee in the mount."—Exodus xxv., 40.

Here is part of the direction to Moses as to detailed arrangements in the Jewish law.

There are two systems of law-making. This of Moses is one. He makes the law according to a certain pattern, which he regards as divine. The whole connects together, part with part of one great system. The other system is generally called the Anglo-Saxon system. It is highly praised, and with some reason, by persons of our race. It simply provides for exigencies as they arise. If an evil exists, a law is passed to correct that evil. Such system as follows is a result which nobody foresaw. With a certain jar and friction, part fits itself to part. In America, we do condescend at the end of a generation to have these laws brought together in one volume, with one index. We call this a revision of the statutes. But, even then we do not change the enactment. We leave it as it was made.

I. I find that this is no peculiarity of law-makers. I observe one class of merchants, who are satisfied if they do what other men in their line are doing, or what they learned to do when they were apprentices. I observe quite another class, who have a theory or idea of what their line of business should be, might be, must be, in our time and place, and are determined in all their doings by this theory or idea. Thus, if I buy a magazine, I can tell whether the compiler were satisfied with accepting certain materials brought to him, and making from them a magazine that will sell; or whether he work from and on an idea, looking to a certain standard in such things which he is determined one day his journal shall attain. So you shall see one school-master, who works along as well as he can to-day, corrects this boy, helps that one forward, quite satisfied, if, as the hour passes, he does the work of an hour; while another has in his mind, even in every detail of the day's routine, a certain theory or ideal of a school, which is indeed a perfect school. The education of these boys shall be, were it only by a shade, better and higher than ever was the education of any boys before. He has had a glimpse, in some mount of vision, of a pattern which God himself might have made. To that pattern he is determined to attain.

Such cases are of every-day remark. Perhaps they do not, from their very familiarity, affect us as the stories of life on a larger theatre. The distinction, when you trace it in war, makes the difference between Napoleon and the generals who opposed him, between Frederic the Great and the Austrian and French marshals. Napoleon has formulated success in the direction, "If you want to take Vienna, take Vienna." If that is your object when the campaign begins, cling to that object; let no other prize tempt you to right hand or left hand. Frederic, even with small armies, always knew what he was fighting for, he knew what he wanted. But the people opposed to him were only trying to defeat him, and had no broader plan of campaign. The result is that in the long-run he succeeds, while in the same long-run they are self-doomed to fail.

II. The distinction thus illustrated is frequently spoken of as the distinction between men of practice and men of native genius. It is supposed that, while the common run of men can be trained in such habits of routine as I have described, only some exceptional men

"Of native impulse, elemental force,"

carve out for themselves courses quite original. I do not think we are to be satisfied with this convenient and easy theory. It is quite too lazy a way, this of accounting for human deficiencies and human successes by the short-hand statement that some people are born to success, and some others to mediocrity. We load with too heavy weight the stars we are born under. A true child of God makes his own destiny. He casts his own horoscope, and places the planets where he will. We shall find that men with very simple native resources achieve great victories, while men with very great native gifts fail miserably. And we are to seek the real distinction, according as the one or the other has a standard of excellence, and is loyal to it or false. Not enough to have such a standard, and then to be craven or fickle. Not enough to bring out the standard on days of parade, and for the rest to keep it laid away in a storeroom. He who, for his own place or calling, will make the picture of possible success; he who will state for himself the true principle of action, and by that principle will lay out the specific methods of procedure,— will have made the beginning for success. The ending will come, as he is loyal or selfish, as he works up to his ideal or forgets it. But without the ideal, without the principle which shall give unity to the separate details, there is no success possible. And when we see — as we do see — a man change all of a sudden from being a mere official, a mere man of affairs, a mere man of routine, to become instead a leader of men, one who points out for his time a new departure and a new success, it is always because that man has of a sudden risen from mere thumb-and-rule life to life controlled by principle. He is at last mastered by an idea!

III. Thus, we have very instructive instances in history, where a statesman who has been trained to routine, and routine only, opens his eyes, perhaps all of a sudden, to some great principle,— larger, broader, deeper than any routine,— and of a sudden breaks all the tangles of his old systems, and stands free in a larger faith. Such an experience is Sir Robert Peel's, who had been trained in the traditions of the Tory party, and had manfully stood for them. He had maintained to the last their theory, that England must produce her own food, and that every possible restriction must be put on the importation of corn. It was almost of a sudden that he owned to his supporters that he had found more light. His future policy was to be based on a great principle, and no longer hampered by traditional methods. It is not simply a change from one method to another. It is an enlargement, from a thing of props and stays and regulations, to a broad, self-explaining, and self-executing policy.

The same experience came to Abraham Lincoln, who held on as long as he could to the fine distinctions which he had drawn in his canvass, as to what he could do and what he could not do, for the slave or for his master. He understood these restrictions, delicate though they were, very precisely. Nor did he ever overstep one of them till the great moment came. Then he assured himself — assured himself, indeed, only after prayer to God, and listening to the voice divine — that there was a great underlying purpose of God to be carried out, which none of those fine distinctions could be permitted to hamper. He gave himself up to this flow of the infinite river of the will of God. He wrote the proclamation of emancipation, which set forward so far God's kingdom on the earth, and, of course, by it he assured the triumph of the constitutional cause.

These instances are sufficient, though they themselves are little in the comparison, to show us the sort of experience which Paul passed through. He could explain with more than subtlety, and with a certain largeness of construction, the old Rabbinical formulas. We see that done to-day so often and so well that it is very easy to imagine Paul attempting it. We see men take up old confessions, and dress them over with nice new dresses, rouge their faces, and trace their eyebrows, so that their own fathers would not recognize the disguised Calvinism. They would deceive the very elect. Paul had, of training and of nature, the gifts which just fitted him for that brightening up and re-presentation of old Judaism. One can imagine him doing it, to the delight of his admirers, the very evening after Stephen died. One can see how readily, to such a man, the rulers in Jerusalem should have given commendations to the rulers in Damascus. Still, all the same, the moment comes for him. You cannot chain a man like Paul, not with golden chains,— no, nor with silken. The moment comes when a higher light flashes on him, and all this ingenuity of construction and interpretation is burned away by the flash. Your Paul stands free. He sees that he can make his own rules and regulations, from the infinite principle which has been revealed to him. To that principle he allies himself. Is it a voice of the Infinite Spirit? His spirit listens, and is in allegiance. All this old *finesse*, all this mosaic of part matched to part, is flung away, as Paul breathes the air, sees the light, and lives the life of freedom.

And a very interesting thing it is to catch glimpses afterwards of Paul's loyal effort to adapt himself to this new light. A careful reader may see that he did not of an instant break up the habits of a life. All the same, he says, he means to do it. "I forget the things that are behind, pressing forward to those that are before," to the measure of the stature of fulness of Christ, even. Great words, but not greater than the things that he was doing. One can imagine them all in that line of training, changing their lives from small and narrow lives, giving up the devices of the old pettiness of Galilee, of Jerusalem, or the school of Gamaliel, and turning to life comprehensive and large. They had the quickening of the illustration of the Life of lives which had passed before their sight, as they went and came with Jesus Christ. Such a man as James, determined that he would tread out the fire which was ready to blaze out on the least provocation; he would be as serene and as constant as his Master. Or such a dreamer as Nathaniel, rousing up from reverie and self-absorption, from counting his own pulse, from looking forward to the redeeming of Israel, and starting out, with the Master's energy, to do something himself for the redeeming of Israel. Or such a man as Paul, tempted, when some one approached him with the old hairsplitting, to reply in the same vein. You get traces of it in those allegories about Hagar in the wilderness, and the rock in the desert. And, all of a sudden, he throws all this by, as a soldier might throw away the elegances of a fencing-master, and with a storm of his Master's own eloquence breaks down all the fine-drawn statements of his opponent. Or such a man as John, as fiery as James, passionate to red heat, calming himself even to the tenderness of the Saviour's own love, and explaining how he does so. Why, we have seen him ourselves! Our ears have heard him, our eyes have seen him, these hands have handled him. Thus is it that we know the Word of Life. In all such instances, they are rising from the details of habits, which at the best must be classed as proper or convenient, into the sweep and sway of lives controlled by the Eternal Spirit.

Let any man try that experiment, who, in the fritter of artificial life, has doubted whether life be worth living. Let any man try it, to whom the machinery or routine of his daily business has become wearing and hateful. Let any boy or girl, coming on manhood or womanhood, try it, if the school-work seems crude and hard, and so is repulsive. What is all this for? That is the question. What is the possible and ideal side of it all? How can these details be brought into the harmonious movement of a great purpose, and that purpose nothing less than the will of God? How can the daily routine of the store, this answering of letters, this measuring of tape, this counting out of buttons, this weighing of mint and anise and cumin as it seems, all be made to play in and "fay in" with the work of prophets, poets, and martyrs? This is it to ask how we can "buckle a shoe" to the glory of God, and how we can "sweep a room" so as to make the action fine. How shall we rise from the degradation of slaves to the dignity of freemen who are sons of God?

It is not by throwing off the duty. Freemen do much more work than slaves do, though, as Dr. Bethune says so well, they do much less labor. To live by the Idea, indeed,— to work in the spirit,— transforms labor, which is the part of brutes and of things, into work with God, as we enter into the order of his universe. And any man gains this sense of emancipation,— he gains the joy and largeness of such work,— who seeks and finds for his daily work the divine measure, plan, and standard. It is in some vision, in which he sees the pattern in the mount. He determines that he will not toil longer on the poor thumb-rule of time. He will work on the scale, proportion, and purpose of eternity.

The man may do the same thing, who is dissatisfied with the social machinery around him. He lives in a village which is as stupid and small as little Pedlington. He lives among people who talk only of things ; and he thinks they select for talk things the most unsavory and perishable. What this will sell for ; how much John got for his farm ; whether Jane did or did not put false dyes into the butter,— such are the staples of conversation. What has such a man to do but to help himself? If he will do that, Heaven will help him. What might this village be? let him ask. Nay, what does God Almighty want it to be? What shall it be — as God lives — when a generation more has gone by? Not hard to answer, these initial qustions, if a man put them resolutely. It shall be a village where the children know something of God's handiwork and his will. They shall know how to love the flowers of the field, the butterfly, the moth, and the dragon-fly, the bird that flies, and the fish that swims. They shall know, in their intercourse with each other, that love is better than hate ; truth better than lying; gentleness better than bullying ; purity better than lust ; the simple word, than the oath profane. Men and women shall find out that society has pleasures and profit such as no loneliness has; that he who lives for the community is the real prince among men ; and that their best life — and that the happiest, too — is life given to the welfare of those around them. "Johns," said one of the world's great benefactors to another, "you

like to make money, so do I. You know how, so do I. But
I have learned one greater pleasure, Johns, than the accumu-
lation. It is the expenditure for the good of my fellow-men."
It does not need a man of millions to teach that lesson, or to
learn it. And my imagined friend, lonely in the dirt and vulgarity of a fishing-village or a deserted pasture-town, may try
this same experiment,— of lifting that place, by the omnipotence of the Spirit, to the ideal plane,— and be certain of
success. For he allies to himself the infinite forces. He
works with God, and God works with him.

Or is it perhaps with yourself that you are dissatisfied?
and this I can well imagine. As the year draws to a close,
you also have considered — as many men like you have considered — what you have cost ; and you have been puzzled,
provoked, nay, distressed, to find you have come to so little.
Mr. Froude has drawn out the picture of you, in a vision he
has painted. Try it for yourself. Range out upon the hillside the cattle which have been slaughtered, that you might
dine ; the sheep who have given their fleeces, that you might
be warm ; array the stokers, the fire-men, the engine-men, who
have driven across the land, by day and by night, the trains
which brought the flour for your daily bread, fine gentleman
that you are.—Ah! there is a bit of horror. I see, on the
sheet yonder, the picture of a poor dog, crushed to death between two freight-cars, as he coupled them. He died ; he
left his children fatherless : because he was at work in the
great combination of industries which feeds me every day.
And yonder is the procession of seamen, of boatmen on
Eastern rivers, of carriers sweating under Eastern suns, and
the groups of swarthy laborers in the mid-day heat of the
tropics, who were set to their toil, that you, and others like
you, should have their coffee, their tea, and their sugar. And
you — what have you done, in the great work of the world?
They have done this for you : what have you done for them?
Well, we all know that our answers to that question are
not satisfactory. What we are does not seem a considerable
result for fifty-seven years, or for forty years, nay, for twenty
years of such contributions from all the world. The debit is
very large, the credit is very small. What then? We can
forget the things that are behind. Yes, and we ought to
forget them,— if we look forward to those that are before. If
• for your own life, you construct the ideal ; if for your own
life, you look for the standard,— pattern in the mount it

is,—divine order of human life. This is what Paul means, when he says he looks forward to that which is before,— to the prize of the mark of the high calling of faith; what he calls, in another place, "the measure of the perfect man."

I suppose that this glimpse, this vision, was what Peter and James and John caught sight of, the day of the transfiguration. Not an accidental sheen of light upon one's garments; but from that day forward the Saviour of men was to them something different than what he had been before. They catch a notion that day, that his life is what God wants man's life to be. This life with God; this self-forget-fulness; this unsleeping vigilance; this eagerness for God's kingdom,— this is the life of a true son of a present God. And you and I, are we not his children? Your life and mine, may these not be ideal? The pattern in the mount, the life God would have us live,— why may not you live by that order? why may not I? He made the beasts to look downward for their food, and that was all. Serpents and their like he made to crawl in the earth, unconscious of all but the dirt around them, not even suspecting to-morrow. But man is born of him, is like him : man may look up even to the heaven, and may make his life even as the life of God.

NOTE.— With the Christmas sermon, "Peace on Earth," this series will be finished. The next series, "From New Year to Midsummer," will begin immediately.

From Thanksgiving to Fast.

FIFTEEN SERMONS

BY

EDWARD E. HALE.

THE GREAT HARVEST YEAR,
LOOKING BACK,
RITUAL,
PRAYER,
RESPECTABILITY,
YOURSELVES
WHAT IT IS TO BE CATHOLIC,
THE JOY OF LIFE,
THE ASSOCIATED CHARITIES,
THE REVISION OF THE BIBLE,
THE BIBLE,
LENT,
NEW LIFE,
BLASPHEMY AGAINST THE HOLY GHOST,
THE FUTURE OF NEW ENGLAND.

Price in paper covers, $1.00; in cloth binding, $1.25.

A second series (of fifteen) of Mr. Hale's sermons is now being issued, of which there have already been printed

THE LIFE IN COMMON,
BODY, MIND, AND SOUL,
BODILY TRAINING,
MENTAL DISCIPLINE,
CANDOR IN THE PULPIT,
SPIRITUAL EXERCISES,
DAILY BREAD,
HAPPY HOMES,
THE SEVENTY RETURNED,
THE LATER PHARISEES,
EMIGRATION TO KANSAS,
BREAD ALONE,
THANKSGIVING,
HEART, MIND, SOUL, AND STRENGTH,
THE PATTERN IN THE MOUNT.

Price, 10 cents per copy, or $1.00 for the series. Published by GEO. H. ELLIS, 101 Milk Street, Boston.

[X V.]

PEACE ON EARTH.

A SERMON

PREACHED AT THE SOUTH CONGREGATIONAL CHURCH,
ON CHRISTMAS DAY, 1879,

BY

EDWARD E. HALE.

BOSTON:
GEORGE H. ELLIS, 101 MILK STREET.
1879.

From Thanksgiving to Fast.

FIFTEEN SERMONS

BY

EDWARD E. HALE.

THE GREAT HARVEST YEAR,
LOOKING BACK,
RITUAL,
PRAYER,
RESPECTABILITY,
YOURSELVES
WHAT IT IS TO BE CATHOLIC,
THE JOY OF LIFE,
THE ASSOCIATED CHARITIES,
THE REVISION OF THE BIBLE,
THE BIBLE,
LENT,
NEW LIFE,
BLASPHEMY AGAINST THE HOLY GHOST,
THE FUTURE OF NEW ENGLAND.

Price in paper covers, $1.00; in cloth binding, $1.25.

A second series (of fifteen) of Mr. Hale's sermons is now being issued, of which there have already been printed

THE LIFE IN COMMON,
BODY, MIND, AND SOUL,
BODILY TRAINING,
MENTAL DISCIPLINE,
CANDOR IN THE PULPIT,
SPIRITUAL EXERCISES,
DAILY BREAD,
HAPPY HOMES,
THE SEVENTY RETURNED,
THE LATER PHARISEES,
EMIGRATION TO KANSAS,
BREAD ALONE,
THANKSGIVING,
HEART, MIND, SOUL, AND STRENGTH,
THE PATTERN IN THE MOUNT,
PEACE ON EARTH.

Price, 10 cents per copy, or $1.00 for the series. Published by GEO. H. ELLIS, 101 Milk Street, Boston.

PEACE ON EARTH.

"On earth peace, good-will toward men."—LUKE ii., 14.

This is the promise of the birth of Christ, as St. Luke and the shepherds interpreted it. Yet even the gospel, at the first blush, seems not to sustain it fully.

"Think not that I am come to send peace on earth," Jesus says distinctly: "I am not come to send peace, but a sword."

And once and again, "There shall be wars and fightings : kingdom shall rise up against kingdom, and nation against nation before the end shall come." All which has certainly proved true.

More remarkable, perhaps, than any text is the distinct and almost exceptional commendation which Jesus bestows upon soldiers who were soldiers by profession. So little is there of the Quaker theory,— that, if no men were trained to war, there would be no fighting. It is in speaking of a professional soldier, an officer in a standing army in a garrison town, that he says, "I have not found such faith, no, not in Israel." It is another officer, in the same standing army, who at the crucifixion says, "Surely this was a righteous man." And yet, again, it is the home of another officer of the same rank in the same army that Peter makes the first great declaration which opens the infant Church to the Gentile world. In face of those three statements in the earliest records, it is impossible for anybody who rests upon those records to take up the extreme view of the non-resistants, that armies are themselves wrong, because war is to be deprecated. If service in an army were in itself a sin in the eyes of Jesus Christ or his apostles, they had occasions of which we know, which would have compelled them to say so.

All the same, it is certain that the drift of the gospel promise is a promise of peace. "Peace be to this house." This is the salutation, not only of the twelve and the seventy in those humble journeys in Galilee, but of every Christian traveller, statesman, or apostle. "And if your peace do not rest upon the house, none the less is it certain that i' shall return upon you." When the end comes,— after the terrible fightings of the preparation, after the visions of the Book of Revelations,— when the end comes, there is to be an end of war; and every man shall sit in peace under his own vine and fig-tree, as Micah promised so long before.

As my contribution to the thoughtful observance of the great festival of to-day, I shall try to show how far this promise has been kept, and what are the lines on which we are to work in trying to fulfil it. We will not look back further than to get help in looking forward. We will look back so far as to see where have been the failures and where the successes. We shall certainly find that we are better off than were the people of that day, though, in literal fact, at the birth of the Saviour,

> " Nor war nor battle sound
> Was heard the world around.
> The idle spear and shield were high uphung,
> The hooked chariot stood
> Unstained with hostile blood,
> The trumpet spake not to the armed throng."

We shall find that on the whole, in the longer arcs of history, the world has made steady progress. I think we shall find the lines on which that progress will be continued.

I. There was no shock of war — nation against nation — when Jesus Christ was born into the world. That fact is fairly claimed as a part of the preparation which a good Providence had made for his coming. Or, to state just the same thing in the modern mechanical fashion, in that fact we find one of the reasons for his success when he came. Before the life of Jesus was ended, this prophecy of peace was over. Clouds were gathering over that clear sky. When he said, "What king, going to make war against another king, sitteth not down first, and consulteth whether he be able with ten thousand to meet him that cometh against him with twenty thousand?" he described exactly what Herod of Galilee ought to have been doing at that moment, in view of the onset of Aretas, his Arab father-in-law. And, soon after the crucifixion, the Galileans, who had lost him whom they called king, received the other shock of Herod's defeat in battle, when he went out to fight against the Arab and his hordes. Still, these were what we call border wars. They did not disturb the course of empire more than the massacre of a few poor Cheyennes, or Modocs or Utes, disturbs the course of empire with us to-day. The war which Christ and the new spirit of life had first to act upon was not public war, but what I might call private battle: such family wars as had made Herod of Jerusalem the murderer of his own children ; so that the Emperor Augustus had said he had rather be Herod's hog than his son. For a Jew must spare a hog's life, but was at liberty to kill as many sons as he chose. This same Augustus, however, is the head of that family of Cæsars in whose domestic life, for the century which then began, there were so many of these murders of children by parents, and husbands by wives, and wives by husbands, that Herod's iniquities in that way were scarcely remarkable. At Roman law, indeed, the father had the right of life and death over his sons and daughters under age, as he had over his slaves.

I should say that the first visible step in legislation and public morals which the new life compelled was the sacredness of human life, which put an end to all these wars within, which ate out the heart of every State. Not to speak of details, the result is very clear. It shows itself all through our modern institutions. The empire of law everywhere takes the place of the old empire of force. The man would be ridiculous to-day who should make any guard against such wickedness as that which, only four centuries ago, killed the royal children of England in the Tower ; or, seven centuries ago, put out the eyes of Prince Arthur first, and murdered him afterward. So completely is it taken for granted that the heads of parties, even, are to respect each other's rights, that under the original plan of our own Government the favorite leader of one party might become the President, and the favorite leader of the other the Vice-President. This was really intended as a convenient arrangement, by the good men who made the Constitution. Accordingly, in 1797, Adams, the head of the Federal party, was chosen President, and Jefferson, the unsuccessful candidate of the Democrats, became Vice-President. That is, he was to be President if the other died. As if you had arranged between Cicero and Catiline that their hatred should be assuaged by making Catiline Cicero's successor. Or as if you settled things between Augustus and Antony, by saying that they must not fight any more, but, when Augustus died, Antony should succeed him ; and meanwhile Antony should live near Augustus, and serve under him. In eighteen hundred years, purely under

6

Christian influences, things have so changed that sensible men seriously adopted that plan as a good plan. Nor did anybody ever think of praising the second person in this arrangement, because he did not conspire to put the first person out of the way. The humanity of the world is in a higher stage. Private war is so far ended ; and so far has the reign of peace begun.

The physical sign of the change — which, as always, came later than its reality — is the utter disuse, in the dress of gentlemen, of reference to war.* So late as President Washington's inauguration, men still wore swords in private society. A dress sword was a part of full-dress costume, as much as a dress fan or a dress hat. True, the sword was a "small" sword. Still it was a sword. The theory behind the fashion was that, in very fact, at his own levee, George Washington might have to "draw and defend himself." The same etiquette is still observed in the presentation of gentlemen to the Queen. The theory of the levee is that some mutinous Jack Cade may attack the palace, and that it may be the duty of these gentlemen in pumps and white stockings to draw these swords of ceremony, and die on the steps of the throne in the defence of their sovereign. But such tags of old etiquette are now mere matters of history. In truth, even the duel is done with. Private war has become preposterous. The man who carries any weapon is ranked as a bully among men of character. This is because society now insists on the protection of human life, though it be the life of a thief or a harlot. And that man is false to the principle on which our social system stands, who takes into his own hand the weapon of assault or of defence. So much is gained.

II. How much is gained as to public war? What has one to say on Christmas morning of such lessons as are taught by beleaguerment by the Affghans of Gen. Roberts in his quarters, as the capture of the "Huascar" after her crew were killed at their guns ; such lessons as Sedan taught, and Sadowa and Solferino, and Gettysburg and Antietam and the Five Forks? How far do these show that peace is coming upon earth, and good will among men?

* Excepting, as a careful friend reminds me, in the two buttons on the back of a gentleman's coat. These peaceful emblems are the "survival" of the buttons which held up the sword belt, so that the weight of the weapon might not drag it down upon the legs. I am afraid I must add — what is a novelty, and not a "survival" — the "pistol pocket." It is true, however, that the pistol carried is too often the bearer's worst enemy.

Well, if I were arguing from statistics,—and I am not,—
I should say that the last century of the United States, including all the horrors of the Civil War, showed in proportion less loss of life in battle than any century of any
nation's history since the world was a world. I should say
that the horrors of the German occupation of France under
Bismarck were as nothing to the horrors of the French
occupation of Germany under Napoleon. I should say that
those invasions were not so terrible as the "Seven Years'
War" half a century before. And then I should say that
the "Seven Years' War" was as nothing in its ruin and
wretchedness compared with the "Thirty Years' War" of
the century preceding. And so I should go back to claim
that steadily, surely, if not rapidly, war, which is barbarism,
has been less barbarous and less, and had imbibed more
and more of Christianity from the beginning. But I do not
regard this observation as central. It merely furnishes a
convenient illustration.

It is clear enough that the Saviour himself does not
regard war in itself as the greatest of evils. He recognizes
the truth that evils may be so great that, in sweeping them
away, war, or something akin to it, shall follow. "It must
needs be that offences come." We are not to expect wars to
cease, till the evils in social orders cease out of which they
are bred. If two men are drunk, the chances are that they
will fight. To make the fighting impossible, we must make
the drunkenness impossible. So if a tyrant oppresses slaves,
it is to be hoped the slaves will revolt. To make revolt
impossible, tyranny must be made impossible. If you have
three million slaves held in slavery by fifty thousand masters, sooner or later civil war must come. If civil war is
to be made impossible, slavery must be impossible. And
we shall find that the great wars of history stand suc-
cessively for some advance of humanity, such as I have
indicated in these successive statements. Once recognize
history as the record of the method of the "Power that rules
for righteousness," and you see why that Power has permitted
war. Our business, on Christmas Day, is not to show that
there has been no war. It is rather to show that war has
not been in vain. And, beside this, we have a right to ask
whether the chances of war are increasing or diminishing.

III. In answer to this question, I observe that one-seventh
part of Christendom—consisting of nearly forty different
nations, as in any old nomenclature they would be calle

— has of its own will united itself in a great Peace Society. It has established a central court, which shall try and settle all disputes among these nations. They have of their own accord disarmed themselves as separate nations, and maintain no military or naval armaments. Of their own accord, their governments leave all negotiations with foreign States to one central authority, the same for all; and, so certain is peace among these forty nations, that this central authority which carries out the injunction of the central court, and the negotiations with foreign powers, is satisfied with an army of twenty-five thousand men, and a navy which is hardly able to keep one frigate in each of the five oceans of the world. The name of this Peace Society is the "United States of America."

I do not forget, nor am I ashamed to own, that this Peace Society once carried on within itself, for four years, one of the most terrible wars in history. No. For that war was, so to speak, essential to the plan. Till that war had been fought, and well fought, no man dared say that the plan was successful. For the men who made this Peace Society dared the great rashness of "uniting five oligarchies with eight republics." * Not till those oligarchies and their kindred were lifted into republics; not till the semi-barbarous barons who controlled them had learned that Christian civilization takes the place of the order of slaves and villains, was the system of the Peace Society possible. That lesson must be taught, was taught. Let us hope that it has been learned, and will ere long be digested. With the learning of that lesson, peace comes.

Now I say that what has been done in the direct Christian order, by one-seventh of the Christian family, is a hint of what is possible among the other six-sevenths. The United States of South America would heal all the political evils under which the separate States of South America pine away and die. And for the future of Europe,— whenever Europe has statesmen who will forecast the future rather than play at jack-straws with the broken fragments of the past,— those statesmen will study this hint, and will reconstruct Europe on some system not dissimilar. This is no dream of a fanatic republican. It is the answer to the prayer of the Saviour of the world, when he prayed for those who came after him, "That they all may be one."

Nearly three hundred years ago, the first statesmen of

* Gouverneur Morris.

Europe were engaged in such a plan for the union of Europe. Henry IV., Sully, Queen Elizabeth and her ministers, thought it not impracticable. It pleased the Society of Jesuits, then as always enemies of peace and liberty, to murder Henry IV., and that scheme fell. Nine years ago on Thanksgiving Day, in this place, I described it, in these words : —

"Of these powers, six were the kingdoms of England, France, Spain, Denmark, Sweden, and Lombardy. Five were to be elective monarchies; namely, the German Empire, the Papacy, Poland, Hungary, and Bohemia. And there were to be four Republics,— Switzerland, Venice, the States of Holland and Belgium, and the Republic of Italy made up somewhat as the Kingdom of Italy is now. These fifteen powers were to maintain but one standing army. The chief business of this army was to keep the peace among the States, and to prevent any sovereign from interfering with any other, from enlarging his borders or other usurpations. This army and the navy were also to be ready to repel invasions of Mussulmans and other barbarians. For the arrangement of commerce and other mutual interests, a Senate was to be appointed of four members from each of the larger and two from each of the smaller States, who should serve three years, and be in constant session. It was supposed that, for affairs local in their character, a part of these senators might meet separately from the others. On occasions of universal importance, they would meet together. Smaller congresses, for more trivial circumstances, were also provided for.

"The plan contemplated a grand army of Europe, of three hundred and twenty thousand men, and a navy of one hundred and twenty vessels, to be provided in quotas agreed upon by the respective members of the association ; and, from the beginning, the members of the association announced that no secession was to be possible or to be permitted.

"With generosity such as few princes have shown, Henry proposed that the executive which should carry out the decisions of the Senate should be the elected Emperor of Germany for the time. This was probably the weakest part of the plan, the point to be secured being of course, then as now, the most difficult. But, as the Emperor was chosen in an assembly in which so many of the several powers had a voice, this seemed the simplest adjustment."

I should not then have dared to say that the war then raging would do what it has done to make real this vision. I doubt if any man would have dared prophesy what has proved true regarding the German Empire as it was then formed. The union in one Empire of the States of Germany has been since made on a plan almost precisely that which Sully and Henry then made for Western Europe. The union of Italy, just before, had been a step in the same direction. For the future, the dream must be that nations which now maintain standing armies of several million men, whose lives are wasted as they fool them away in garrison, shall agree to disarm. They must make a common tribunal, and they must give a central power the means of enforcing its decisions. This is the dream. Human selfishness and human experience now unite in suggesting it with the eternal demand of the gospel of peace.

So much right has one to say that it is nearer than ever.

IV. But, to bring all this about, the Saviour never relied upon human selfishness or human experience, upon the wisdom of statesmen, the prudence of economists, or the experience of history. No. He said distinctly, "God has hid these things from the wise and prudent, though he has revealed them unto babes." He has chosen the foolish things of the world to confound the prudent. He has chosen things that are not to confound the things that are.' It is in happy homes that the spirit is to grow which shall teach statesmen at last that all that government exists for is that homes may be happy. It is in peaceful lives that the spirit is to be bred, which shall at last sway Parliaments and Reichstags, and Corteses and Assemblies, till rulers shall see that war is a fashion of the past, and peace the fashion of the future. It is as men seek God more in their own lives, and find him in such seeking, that nations begin to know that he is the God of nations as he is the God of men. So it is that the appeal of him who is born this day was not first made to kings or armies. It is made in the squalor of the inn at Bethlehem ; it is made in the festivity of the wedding at Cana ; it is made in the cheerfulness of the evening meal at Bethany ; it is made at the family gathering, when he summons his own to eat with him the passover. "Peace be to this house," they say. And the fruit is, "Peace to this nation." Peace be in my heart and yours. And from that seed, lo! thirty, sixty, and a hundred fold. The morning light breaks. The shepherds, shivering and chilled, are afraid to trust their eyes; but, all the same, the light does break, though it is so slow. Yes, and it gains on the darkness, gray and pearly. The old stars, sacred to fight, are paling out. I do not see Orion's sword. I cannot see Bootes's club. I do not see the Lion any more. The sky is all warm and aglow. Warmer and brighter! And at last, one dazzling Ray, and then the Sun! the Sun!

The Sun of Righteousness has come!

There is a new heaven and a new earth!

The former things are passed away!

Note.— At the moment when this sermon was preached, I had not read Prof. JOHN FISKE's instructive syllabus of a course of lectures on "Evolution in History." That syllabus was printed but not then published, I believe. I am glad to refer readers of intelligence to it now; for I could not find higher authority to confirm my view, as stated above, as to the possible — may I not say probable? — pacification of Europe.

FROM NEW YEAR TO MIDSUMMER.

The publication of the next series of Mr. Hale's sermons will begin at once. Each sermon will be printed and delivered to subscribers in the week after it is preached. The sermons will be sent by mail, postpaid, to any part of the country.

Subscription, $1.00 for the series of twenty sermons.

Address

GEO. H. ELLIS, Publisher,

101 Milk Street, Boston.

[XVI.]

·EXAGGERATION.

A SERMON

PREACHED AT THE SOUTH CONGREGATIONAL CHURCH,

BY

EDWARD E. HALE.

BOSTON:

GEORGE H. ELLIS, 101 MILK STREET.

1880.

EXAGGERATION.

"Let your communication be *yea, yea,* and *nay, nay;* for whatever is more than this cometh of evil,"— ἐκ τοῦ πονηροῦ ἐστιν. — MATT. v., 37.

The rule is violated in our time, first by the passion for exaggeration, and yet again by a curious counter-habit,— by the pretence of indifference, and a consequent under-statement.

It is said that the exaggeration is an American habit, and that we borrow the indifference — the pretence of not caring — from the English. I do not know if either of these statements is true.

It is true, that the immense physical measurements of a new country like this give a certain emphasis, sometimes ludicrous, sometimes grand, to its exaggerations. There have come into our local language some national phrases, which belong to these enormous measurements. Such are the expressions "all out-doors," "all creation," and others more local, and perhaps less sonorous. The truth is that the English language, when transferred from an island to a continent, often has to be stretched for the mere physical purposes of the new measurement. Thus the English word "pond" originally was the same as a "pound,"—a small enclosure of water. But here it applies itself to tracts of water like Sebago Pond, larger than all the lakes of the English lake region put together; while the word "lake," in turn, is applied to inland seas. The word "field" meant to an English farmer an enclosure which he walked across in a few minutes, where he directed his laborers by his voice, and which, probably, with a handful of men, he harvested in a day. When a farmer in California, or in Iowa or Minnesota, applies the same word to an enclosure six miles long and six miles wide, around which his reaper proceeds once in twelve hours, changing horses at certain way-stations, that the work may be more swiftly done, the old word does not fully express his meaning ; and, in the course of his talk, certain expletives come in,— such as a "bonanza farm,"— which, in the end, affect the method of his language. The farmer's boy in New England gratifies his literary longing — while the storm howls and the snow drifts out doors — by lying on the floor, in the long evening, and reading, by a pine knot, of William Cowper's Winter's Walk : —

> "The cattle moan in corners where the fence
> Screens them, ...
> . . . . . And there they wait
> Their wonted fodder. . . . . . Silent, meek,
> And patient of the slow-paced swain's delay."

The boy wonders where his father's cattle would be, were they left all night under such shelter as a fence would give them ; and when he reads of the winter's snow as simply a plaything for the dog,

> " Who snatches it .
> With ivory teeth or plows it with his snout,"

while the swain trudges on without noticing it, the boy is wondering how he should describe in stately verses his own morning's walk on snow-shoes, high above the fields and the fences. When he does come to the inevitable moment when in young life we try poetry, his language — it is of course, I believe — takes on a certain stilted over-statement. We notice this habit most, when we are a little away from home. Travel at the West, and you are told in one place that here is the largest beer-vat " in the world " ; in another, that here is the largest manufactory of tubs " in the world " ; in another, that this is the largest establishment for packing pork " in the world." The West always measures itself against " the world." I am by no means sure that we have not the same habit here, only we do not notice it. I think I could find speeches and reports which speak of our schools as the best " in the world," our prisons the finest " in the world," our streets the cleanest " in the world." Only last week, I had to stop in two different shops, neither of them large, in waiting transfer for street-cars. Curiously enough, in one of them was sold the coldest soda " in the world," and in the other the best cream soda " in the world." Such fortunate chance enabled me in the same half-hour to stand in two places so exceptional.

This habit of exaggeration has come to be recognized as a special element of American humour. The English especially, who have very little of it, excepting when they are blaming themselves, treat of Artemus Ward, Mark Twain, and the circle of humorist authors, as if a knack at exaggeration were their principal faculty. Indeed, it is probably true that exaggeration is the essential element of all caricature.

The counter habit of under-statement is said to be borrowed from the English. It is also said to be local here in Boston and the neighborhood ; and it is thought to indicate a lack of vitality, resulting from one-sided systems of education. I do not regard it as very important. If I were preaching in any place twenty miles from here, I should not allude to it. But here I like to caution you younger people against a local absurdity.

It is in the affectation of indifference. As when I ask you if you have been to the Mechanics' Fair, and you say, "No," really you did not think it worth while, of course it was nothing to Philadelphia, and after Vienna of course who would want to go, and then in the next breath turn to say how dull Boston is, and wonder how people can live here. Or I ask you if you enjoyed the play last night; and you say : "Oh, it was all very well. Of course it was not good, but it was not even bad enough to be entertaining." You came away before it was over, and do not know why you went at all. Or I ask you how you spent your summer ; and you tell me that you stayed at the mountains as long as you could, but really the people were so vulgar that it was a sad bore ; and then you went to Newport, but there was nothing going on there, and it was terribly tedious, and then you came home. Satire and ridicule easily show that this languor and pretence of indifference are very absurd. It is my business just now to show that this pretence, like the pretences of exaggeration, are very wicked.

I. "Let your communication be yea, yea, and nay, nay." This is the rule of the Sermon on the Mount. "Whatever is more than this cometh of evil." It is well worth our remark that Jesus Christ, who generally dwells on the inner spirit of an action, on its motive and principle, here occupies himself on the method, on the outside act, as if this were too important in this case to be passed by. The truth is that the habit of expression reacts on the man who speaks. The habit of exaggeration in speech distorts the observation, and makes the conscience itself unreliable. And this other habit of under-statement, this pretended lassitude, which began only in the thought that it is genteel to be interested in nothing, ends in making the temper as languid as it pretends to be. I am old enough to have seen the whole progress in a generation, in the writers for the public press, of a habit of over-wrought statement, akin to what was called Euphuism in the days of Elizabeth. I am sorry to say that this habit was caught by the newspaper men from that distinguished member of their craft, Charles Dickens. It was one of the amusing jokes of his earlier style to use pompous, long words, instead of simple, short ones. Thus:—

"Bob Sawyer and his very particular friend applied themselves most assiduously to the eatables before them." This is instead of "ate voraciously." So:—

"The breakfast ripened into a state of extreme facetiousness."

"The majority of the inhabitants direct their energies to the letting of fashionable apartments." In Dickens's own hands, this burlesque is always guarded. You are almost told that it is burlesque. Nothing is more frank and simple than his writing where there is no joke of this sort implied. But this play with long words became so easy to imitate, that the very weakest reporters of the press took it up. And now you do not read that John Smith was called before the court. You read that "an inebriated individual, who answered to the familiar appellation of Smith, was summoned to give an account of himself." I am sorry to say that the pulpit is sometimes as guilty as the press. A distinguished preacher, now not living, could not say,—

"Jesus went to Jerusalem."

When he wanted to say that, he would say,—

"The founder of our religion was proceeding to the metropolis of his country."

II. Now you will not suppose that I cite such falsities in language as if we had any concern here with literary usage or criticism. It is the moral depreciation which follows, where men thus traverse the Saviour's rule: it is this which we must consider. The man is in a bad way,—morally,—who is learning the trick of using words larger than the occasion. That game of brag reacts, and, like the old

Congreve rocket, is apt to hurt most the man who uses it.
And exactly as your first instruction to a young sportsman is
that he do not overcharge his gun, lest he hurt himself more
than he hurt the birds, so the first instruction to a young
writer for the press is that he leave out his exaggerated
epithets, lest he do himself an irremediable injury. When I
was in training for such duties, at sixteen years of age, I
handed a notice of a magazine to my chief. He gave it
back to me, saying it would answer when I had struck out all
the " verys." I had said that it was " very good," and would
be read by a "very large" number of people, who wanted
"very much " such entertainment. I often think of his criticism, as I read the work of young journalists. I long to say,
" Are you sure you mean what you have written ? " When
you say every one in Boston should hear Miss A. B. read
Shakspere, do you really mean that three hundred audiences,
of a thousand each, including all the Portuguese and Italians
at the North End, all the idiots from the retreat, all the
babies in arms, shall go every day for ten months to listen
to the lady. When the newspaper says that Mr. X. Y. Z.'s
book on the Constitution should be in every family in the
country, does it really mean that three or four of the largest
printing-offices in the country shall be engaged, night and
day, for the next year, in printing copies of it to meet this
demand for an edition of seven million. Not only does the
press lose its own influence by this carelessness of exaggeration, but the men who write are all the time losing the
nicety of their own discrimination between truth and error.
And the editor-in-chief, who reprimands a subordinate for
reporting a meeting which he never attended, or giving a
sketch of a speech which was never delivered, may well
ask himself whether he never instructed that same man to
write up a book or to write down a cause. He may well
consider how far he is himself responsible for the gradual
decline of the newspaper in general estimation.

III. It is said, when men press the doctrine of the Sermon
on the Mount, that all social intercourse hinges on tenderness and civility of language. It is said that we should
make each other very unhappy, if we told the whole truth ;
and that that is really good breeding which bids a man say
he is glad to see a visitor, when he is not ; or which asks a
man to come again, whom you would be glad never to see.
On *white lies*, as these civil falsehoods are called, much

has been written, and very ingenious defences have been made for them. They play a very important part in our training,— far too important for me to neglect them here.

1. And first, though not chiefly, I have to say that the commonplace excuse exaggerates fearfully the necessity of white lies, even on the vulgar, worldly statement. One of the highest dignitaries of the English Church said to me that he heard his servant say he was not at home. " I was in my shirt-sleeves," he said, " on a step-ladder, hanging a picture. I leaped down. I ran into the hall. I astonished both my footman and my visitor by saying, ' I am at home. How dare you say I am not at home! But, as you see, madam, I am not dressed to receive company, and am very much engaged. ' " I think that particular white lie was never told again in the Deanery of Canterbury, while that clergyman lived. I remember very well how a single man — of simple and even quaint habits — changed the whole fashion of a large circle of young people around him. He out-Quakered the Quakers in the simplicity of his statement. He carried his eagerness for the spoken truth to what seemed to me the fine absurdity of fanaticism; for such absurdity is possible. He read in the newspaper one day that, if the old copper cent lacked a little dot in the centre, it was counterfeit. Unwilling to circulate false money, he accumu-lated a great heap of such coins before it occurred to him to ask whether the statement itself were true ; and it proved not to be. But, for all this, the simple truth of that man affected all of us. His mere presence in our companies made us careful of saying we were glad when we were not glad, or that we hoped for things we did not hope for. And my young friends who will squarely try the gospel rule of this text will certainly find that it does not press so hardly as the hand-books of etiquette, and other treatises on white lying, pretend it does.

A much more important remark is this, that the white lie reveals a falsehood in the speaker's heart, which he is trying to conceal. It is there that the remedy must be applied.

On your comfortable, cheerful evening,— when you have finished your day's work, and have your game of whist, your novel, or other provided entertainment in hand,—there comes in this stranded, lonely, forlorn, old companion, whom you have asked to come when he will. You greet him with a false smile. You say you are glad to see him, when you wish he were at the end of the world. You tell squarely a white lie.

Yes. But trace that to the bottom. Where is the falsehood? It is not your word which is to blame. The word is saying what ought to be true, what in your soul you know ought to be true. You ought to be glad to see him. You are prosperous, he is unfortunate. You live in society, he is lonely. You have a home, he has none. And both of you are God's children. God has given to you these comforts, these luxuries; and for what? That you should fatten on them alone? No! But that you should share them with others. What you would say, if you told the truth, would be, "I ought to be glad to see you,"—for you ought. In truth, you are making a struggle with yourself. Your tongue is pleading that the selfishness of the heart may not be known.

And, to cure this evil of social falsehood, society must go deeper than it goes in crudely satisfying itself by telling disagreeable truths. Let society be rid of the false life beneath, which needs to be concealed. Let society understand and feel that men are in the world to bear each other's burdens, and not to mope and dose and guzzle, nor to try to enjoy alone. When society has cured the falsity of the heart, there is no danger that the lip will have any thing to conceal.

The classical defence of the hollowness of white lies, as a social necessity, was made, near a hundred years since, in the celebrated novel called the " Castle of Truth." It is well enough to consider the circumstances of that defence, and to see what has come of it in the century as it has gone by.

In the most false court of the most false period of the world's history, the celebrated Madame de Genlis, the teacher of Louis Philippe, afterward the King of France, put forth this plea for silver falsehood, for the falsities of society. She supposed, for the instruction of the young prince, the existence of a magic castle where every one should be compelled by the charm which surrounded him to speak that which was in his heart. And she represented its inmates as in constant strife in consequence: they said unkind things, and received unkind answers. And the moral she drew for her princely pupil was that the truth must not always be told, that for the grace of society and its ease there must be false expressions on a thousand lips!

Melancholy lesson! That was not the true lesson! The true lesson needed no fairy tale to teach it! That man's heart, as man trains it, is not so innocent that its every throb shall be beautiful! That in France, in those days of France, there was scarcely a thought in the polished society of France which was worthy of revealing,—which was not poisoned, barbed, and wicked. A lesson which, ten years after, the Revolution in France taught with a frightful emphasis to the world. The young prince was taught that the hearts around him were so false that the revelation of their true throbbings would be terrible : that to speak the truth easily, he must be a true man, — true in heart, true in thought, true in feeling. The right thought will not want for the right utterance, nor fear it. And, when the true tale of the true Castle of Truth shall be written, its moral shall be this : The magic of that castle shall open every breast to every eye, because in every heart there shall be something worth looking on. The Castle of Truth shall show men whose lives are true, and there will need no magic then to make their voices true. It shall show that he who has no unchristian thoughts will speak free as air, and not pain for a moment the humblest of his hearers. It shall show that the jewel truth is beautiful on every side, that it needs no setting to change its beauty or its lustre, no contrast to add to its charm. When the world shall have advanced in its training, when it shall demand brothers with sisters to *be* true, when it shall claim that the heart beat truly, that the hands work truly, that the thought resolves truly, then it shall see that always, though heaven fall and earth yawn open, the *lips* may *speak* truly.

How well the prince learned that lesson, France and its history shows to-day. It so happened that in what was wittily called the rivalry of the Weathercocks, after the fall of Napoleon, this Orleans family came to the front, as in so many disturbances in France before, as the rivals of the Bourbons. It so happened that this prince, trained in this gospel of white lies, the prince of posture-masters as he proved himself, won the confidence of the French Liberals so often deceived ; and, in the Revolution of 1830, they made him their king. He was to be the people's king,—not the king of France, as the Bourbon had been, but the king of the French, because they had chosen him. Of which the end is best described in those bitter words of Lafayette, which will be this king's epitaph in history, " He has lied to us." In eighteen years, France learned the falsity of the lies, white, black, silver, and golden, which he told them. At the end of that time, Paris drove him away, as it drove away the Bourbon before him. And now the princes of his line are exiles, plotting for that throne, of which Thiers has said, "There is but one throne, and there are three claimants." As they plot, and while they wait, they may well study again the "Castle of Truth," consider what training the last king of France had in his boyhood, and what has come of it.

That honeyed sophistry of the courts, and the verdict which history has rendered on it, ought to teach us all the true lesson and train us to its duties.

For that training, the first lesson is that we begin ; that our communication be yea, yea, and nay, nay. We will not imagine cases of casuistry. We will not lapse into the languor of affected indifference. We will not be lured into the burlesque of extravagance. We will not, on the other hand, conceal honest feeling. What the heart feels, the lip shall speak. What the head knows, the lip shall tell. What is doubtful and vague, of that we will be silent. Yes for yes, no for no !

Whatsoever is more than this comes from the devil.

FROM NEW YEAR TO MIDSUMMER.

A new series of Mr. Hale's sermons, to consist of twenty began with the New Year. The following have been already, published : —

TIME AND GRIEF.
THE CENTENNIAL OF THE CONSTITUTION.
PUBLIC WORSHIP.
AGGRESSIVE CHRISTIANITY.
MARY MAGDALENE.
THE SHIFTLESS.
GOD'S LOVE.
WHERE WILL SECT GO?
CONSCIENCE AND WILL.
EXAGGERATION.

Each sermon will be printed and ready for delivery in the week after it is delivered in the pulpit.

Subscription, $1.00 for the series of twenty.

Series No. 1. FROM THANKSGIVING TO FAST,
Series No. 2. FROM FAST TO CHRISTMAS,

are ready for delivery. Price, $1.00 each, in paper covers; $1.25 in cloth binding.

Address

GEO. H. ELLIS, Publisher,

101 Milk Street, Boston.

MARY MAGDALENE.

Dove)

A SERMON

PREACHED IN THE SOUTH CONGREGATIONAL CHURCH,

BY

EDWARD E. HALE.

BOSTON:

GEORGE H. ELLIS, 101 MILK STREET.

1880.

MARY MAGDALENE.

Mary called Magdalene, out of whom went seven devils.— LUKE viii., 2.

THE New Testament theory of possession by devils is by no means clear, and probably is not meant to be. This is clear enough, however, that the devils, whatever they were, hunted in groups or troops. That is the custom of all devils known to us now, and there is some advantage in studying them together. Possibly we may come upon the laws of their association.

Nothing whatever is known of this Mary but what is told in the text and in the accounts of the Saviour's crucifixion and resurrection. We know that she was the companion of Joanna, the wife of Herod's treasurer. The assumption that she was a woman who had been an adultress is wholly without foundation in Scripture. All that we know is that she had lived in Magdala, a town near the Saviour's home in Capernaum ; that she, with her friend, Joanna, who was a lady in rank, ministered to him in his Galilean journeys ; that she saw him at the crucifixion and after his resurrection. We know this, and that seven devils had gone out from her. What those seven devils may have been we are left to imagine from what we know of the lives of women of her time and of ours.

Whatever her life was, it is certain that in that time this Mary had grown to womanhood, secluded rather more from open life and intercourse with boys and men than if she had grown up with us, but not in the absolute seclusion of an Eastern harem to-day. When the time for her marriage came, the friend of the bridegroom came to treat with her father and her mother, to ask their permission for the marriage. But this by no means implies that the bridegroom had not seen her and selected her, nor that she did not love him or select him among other suitors. They had been betrothed, he and she, in a solemn ceremony of betrothal. When the time of the wedding came, the bridegroom with his family and friends came in a brilliant procession through the streets to her house. Her maidens had dressed her, had veiled her, had crowned her, and her procession was in waiting. When the bridegroom's procession arrived, it took her procession in, and escorted her and her train to his house. There he unveiled her, and in this act the ceremony of marriage ended. Then followed a festival, lasting, perhaps, through many days of feasting, dancing, and rejoicing. Of this festival, of course, the bride was chief. And it was not, perhaps, for a fortnight that she was left to her husband and her home.

And then, so left, I have fancied that this bride may have felt the reaction from courtship, betrothal, and festival. I do not know what her husband was. One of those lake fishermen, perhaps, off for two or three days at a time perhaps, waiting for a catch, following the whims of a school of fish, or carrying in those caught to sell to the garrison at Tiberias. When he came home,— well, the wet, dirty fisherman's gear was not exactly the costume of the wedding night. He was tired and silent, and cross, perhaps; at the best, when he told his experiences, they were not all tales of flutes and myrtles and roses and nightingales. And, with the morning, he would be away again. I have fancied that the home at Magdala may have seemed narrow, dull, and dead; that she did not like the neighbors, good enough fish-wives, perhaps, but not comparing well with the school companions of her mother's home. I have fancied that, as she sat and spun and wove, or perhaps as she cleaned fish and spread them to dry on the beach, she looked backwards, not with regret exactly, but with a comparison which did not make the present attractive, and that on any dull day she looked forward gloomily to three hundred and sixty-five such days in a year, and to ninety such years, if, by ill luck, she lived as long as Sarah did. That is, I have imagined that the first devil which haunted the home and life of this young bride was the Devil of Discontent. She was married, but marriage was not the delightful wonder which prattling girls had thought it. She was mistress of her own home. But to reign in the house of a fisherman was not the gorgeous empire she had dreamed of. Poor child! she did not know how to command her circumstances; and so this mean Devil Discontent came sneaking in and ruled her.

And no such devil is satisfied to remain long alone. So I have fancied that, in the restlessness of this life, she tried, in an uneasy way, to wriggle out of her wretchedness, by seeking outside her house that excitement which she could not find in the routine within. Did she, perhaps, think she could

show to those mean-spirited women who surrounded her at
Magdala the superior ways, the style, and adornment of
the gentlefolk at Capernaum or of Tiberias; that she could
show them something of the propriety and elegance which
she had noted when her mother took her on a visit to her
mother's cousin, the chief contractor for the garrison? Did
she bring out the bravery and finery of dresses which had
been hidden away since the wedding? Did she make frequent journeys to the bazaar at Capernaum, and reinforce
those scanty stores with new equipments, so that on some
brilliant Sabbath in the spring she could astonish all her
side of the synagogue with the new wonders of her raiment,
more gorgeous than Solomon's, and draw the curious looks
and admiration of the men upon the other side? Did the
loom rest and the distaff stand unused while she made time
for these new devisings? And so did she appear, first on the
Sabbath days, then on other festivals, the woman of most
brilliant dress in all Magdala? Did she make time, money,
comfort all bend to this new passion for adornment? Did
the Devil Discontent find new field for indignation when this
passion was not gratified? Then we may safely say that he
had been reinforced in his empire over the poor bride by the
arrival of the other devil, of Display.

And, when these two devils are at work with the poor
child, one knows very nearly what devils they will bring in
to help them. For so soon as home and its poor, humble
life are squarely compared in her mind with this showy life
of fashion, though it were only the fashion of Magdala, there
come in cravings for the grander life of the more showy
women, whom poor Mary thinks more fashionable, of Tiberias and Capernaum. There comes in the pitiful wish to
talk about this person and about that, for whom a year ago
she did not care a straw,— as certainly she never thought of
them. Ignorant of matters of real interest, she and persons
as shallow as herself meet now at the village well, now at
the sea-shore, now in the market-place, only to discuss the
lives, the manners of others, their successes and their failures.
If the child of Dorcas is born under an evil eye or not, if it
is true that the prefect sent back to Zebedee a boat-load of
fish because they were not fit to use, what was the message
with which Michael's boy was charged when the centurion
sent him across the lake to Gadara, whether it could be
true that the contract of marriage was broken off between
Levi and Elizabeth,— this tittle-tattle of the market-place, .

exaggerating every fault and shrouding every virtue with a blemish, comes in across the old simple current of a good girl's maiden life. The common interests of home all give way, and even her thoughts are no longer her own ; for they come and go as these devils will, and *she* thinks that they all talk of falsehoods and intrigues and impurities. It is not when she is with others only, it is quite as much when she is alone, that, beside the devils Discontent and Display, the chattering devil whom I shall call the Devil of Gossip, claims her as his slave.

And then, where there is so much talk, so much vanity and so much vain talk, another devil comes. It will not do to take any step backward. We must keep up to the proud pre-eminence we have won in style, in dress, in conversation, and in all these other little arts of the gay world of the lakeside. We live to shine. We live to please in that gay circle of the upper ten of Magdala ; and no other competitor must come between poor Mary and the success which she has attained. She must please by this art here, and by that art there ; for the poor creature thinks now that people are to be pleased only by effort to please them. In the early days, just after the marriage festival, or perhaps in days before it, she pleased Alphæus best simply by telling him what was, what sweet thoughts crossed her pure mind and what fine feelings crossed her pure heart. But all men are not as easily pleased as Alphæus, nor, alas! all women, she says. And so she says one thing here, and alas ! quite another thing there. Here is an old friend of her father's, who cannot bear to see her throwing life away and on some festival he takes her a little away from the dancers to give her a little caution. And she cannot resist the temptation just to fascinate him also. And to him she tells her pretty penitences so sweetly, and explains her temptations so artlessly, and asks his advice so simply, that she supposes, little fool, that she has deceived the very elect. And when, within fifteen minutes after, when the turn in the dance brings her in with Hiram, her husband's early friend, who was away with the army when they were married, there is just a drooping of the eye, and just a little start when he speaks, and just a sentence half begun and not finished, which shall imply what of course she must not say,— that if,— well, what is done is done,— but if Alphæus had gone away with the soldiers, and Hiram had stayed at home, well, things might not have been what they are. And, in ten minutes more, as they

are all sitting at the entertainment, and the young Roman
standard-bearer Lucius makes a chance to speak, in broken
Syriac, some words of clumsy compliment to the young Hebrew matron, why, you would have said, in turn, that he was
the only person whom she ever respected or cared for. The
very Devil of Falsehood himself has got hold of this girl, who
was as true as the light when Alphæus took her from her
mother's home,— so certain is that devil to find entrance
where the Devils of Discontent and Display and Slander
have led the way.

They came in the suite of discontent. But discontent is
rampant as ever, although they have come in. No change in
her home, no change in circumstance, drives him away. This
poor woman cannot make herself the queen of circumstance.
She cannot make circumstance serve her. Her children
come to her, but she cannot reconcile herself to the care and
confinement and change of life they bring. Her husband
can make nothing of the change of life which has come in,
with the madness of possession by all these devils; and she,
of course, does not analyze her life. All that she knows is
that she is more discontented than ever. The gayeties of
life have not satisfied her; brilliancy and jollity have not
satisfied her; gossip and lying do not satisfy her. What
those who look on see does not suggest itself to her. They
see that, with the tight sway of all these devils choking her
and hindering her, she is no longer the light-hearted girl
whom Alphæus loved. She is no longer the free, proud
woman who deserved his love. She has no thought for him
now,— nay, no real thought for her children. She has no
thought for any but herself. All this gossip about the frail-
ties and follies of other people betrays no interest in them.
No : if you would really interest her, you must talk now
about her,— about her jewels, her dancing, her success at
the picnic, her repartee to the publican. It is " I by myself
I " who is the queen of poor Mary's reverence. For the
other devils all together have made a throne which the
Devil of Selfishness is sitting on.

And then she begins to be aware how she herself is
changed. She, who was the lightest-hearted girl in Magdala,
the sweetest-tempered, the favorite of all the other girls, is now
wayward and cross, and she knows she is. It is not only that
the old, simple pleasures have lost their charm. If Alphæus
serenade her with his flute on the anniversary of her birthday, she is provoked, and not pleased. She is not pleased

with anything but sheer compliment: she is provoked with everything in its turn. She is not pleased when she is left alone, she is not pleased when the children come storming round her, she is not pleased when she has driven them away. Is it ill-health? She tries to think so. But the village doctor cannot find that anything is the matter with her. The symptom is a symptom which sometimes announces bodily weakness. But this time it is something worse than a bodily crisis. Poor creature! It is not her body, it is not her mind which is weak and faint. It is the soul itself which is all awry, so beset with devils. It is the Devil of Irritability which has possession of her.

And then some devil, perhaps all the other devils together, tempt her to drive him out. And she is just foolish enough to suppose that this is only nervousness and faintness: it is a something physical perhaps, something which, maybe, all women have to undergo. Perhaps she is ill. And one of these fools she has been flirting with sends to her, under some pretence, a little skin of the wine of Eshcol, making his sister bring a message that it is recommended by high authority at Jericho. And then her poor husband, Alphæus, is only too glad to bring, on his next trip, other medicines of the same sort, such as the wives of the officer of Tiberias drink when their nerves fail them. And, more and more, the irritable, selfish, discontented woman seeks the refuge which sleep gives, if nothing else will give, and which wine promises to give, even if it often breaks its promise. And here is an old hag from behind the mountains, who is willing to explain to her what are the "drugged wines" which the Scripture warns her against in forty places. Of course she would not take them, if she were not ill! Never! But, as she is, one has to take so much the less of these. It is only a little of the Eshcol wine mixed with the seeds of the poppy. See, Mary Magdalene can do it herself if she will, from the poppy-seeds in her own garden. If she will! Ah me! will was gone long ago. She is sure to do it so soon as the tempter speaks to her. It is no true lover like her husband. It is not even a false lover like him who sent her that false gift. It is the very king devil of all the devils,— Belial,— the devil of lust, of intemperance, of self-indulgence, who has got possession of her now. There is no reasoning now. There is no poor excuse of self to self. "I want to do it. Therefore I do it. I choose to do it." So it is. Prayer is gone, duty is gone, faith is gone, hope is gone, all is gone, save self and license and indulgence. No, not all; for discontent is sti'l here, the wretch'ed love of display is here, the same false tongue is here, the same spirit of slander! But all save these is gone. Her house was empty. But it is not empty now. These seven devils, e'ch worse than he who came before, have entered in and dwell there. They possess her—poor creature, poor sot forsaken!—for their own.

Devils worse than the first, indeed!

Now it is as easy to trace the oth r part of that history. Such a woman as that does not take any rest or satisfaction in her position. No : you say she has made her own lot. So she has. But it does not follow that she likes it. To man or woman, so broken down by the devils of self-indulgence, you go, who were, perhaps, never so tempted. You go with your Joseph Surface talk about their wretchedness and the misery of their fall, and you find that they can talk about it, if that were all, much more terribly than you can. They know all about it. Na', they are clutching at any straw for succor. Suppose such a woman as I have described, unable even to maintain the appearances of home, not fit to be trusted with her own children even,—she sees them withdrawn from her,—she knows that her husband cares for her only as he would care for any other wreck, left upon him as a part of his duty to provide for. She wakes every morning, to wish to God that it were evening; and she goes to a wretched bed at night, to wish to God that it were morning. She does not need any exhortation of yours to know how deep is the gulf into which she has fallen.

No ; but it is easy to see how such a woman as that heard the words which the Saviour of men first of all addressed to such women and to such men. First, it is easy to see how at Capernaum, at Tiberias, or at Magdala, such a woman as that, living for excitement, and always eager to see what the crowd saw, would be sure to be in the throng that surrounded him. Why, she would have been there, were this an Arab chief who had ridden into the village, or a Roman sergeant with his soldiers. Then, once in his presence, it is easy to see how she would follow him, to hear everything and to see everything. A poor straw upon the wind, like her, who has lost all personal self-direction, obeys and cannot help obeying a leader like him, who personifies will, whose will is act, who wills and does, nor even speaks but with that authority which of course commands.

Imagine her, wretched, broken, hating herself and hating life, imagine her lying on the hillside, wondering why she came among all those people who look at her so distrustfully, and yet compelled to hear him speak, when he says : —
"Come unto me ye who are weary and heavy-laden, and I will give you rest."
Of course she listens to see what more he has to say to her.
"Take my yoke upon you and learn of me ; for I am meek and lowly of heart, and ye shall find rest unto your souls."
Rest ! Why, he knows just what she is craving. He never saw her, but he knows better than she what is the matter with her. You do not wonder that, even if the crowd disperses, she follows him. You do not wonder, if when she sees his confidence in her, she pours out the whole wretched story of her life,— her discontent, her folly, her falsehood, and the ways of her throwing herself away. No ; and you know what he will say.
He will say, "Daughter, thy sins are forgiven thee." She is not to be champing at that bit any longer. She is not to be harping on that old string. "Let the dead bury the dead," he will say. "Thy sins are forgiven thee, wiped clean out of the book of God's remembrance."
"And I, Lord ? "
You are to begin anew. Turn round. Be born again. Forget yesterday, excepting as you mean to do differently from yesterday. To-day's life is a new life. You have been serving seven devils, you say. Now serve God. Here is his kingdom ! Serve him now.
Before that will of his and before his command, those seven devils give way, and leave her — for a time. If only they do not come back, as devils will, to an empty house,— empty, swept, and garnished. But he does not mean that. And she — as the first new germ of will begins to shoot up under the sunlight of God's love — she does not mean that. That life is not empty, shall not be empty. To serve God is easier than to serve the devil, under the magic of her Master's will. To find some outcast more wretched than she herself, and in a lower deep than she, and to bring her also to his presence ; to look for that leper, and give food and nursing and courage there ; to be a mother to those orphans, who have been left without a friend ; to fill life full with the services which he begins, and which with the instinct or contagion of love she knows how to follow up upon,— all this

crowds full her days. Yes : to take her own children back to
the home which is bright again. How could it have seemed
cheerless? To make that home the shrine and palace of
every joy and benediction for every child and man and
woman in Magdala,— how could that ever have seemed a
trifle? Life is all crowded full with living now. Night is
blessed with sleep, and day is blessed with love. Morning,
noon, and night, she asks, and all her household ask, where
is he to-day who has wrought for us this marvel? Morning,
noon, and night. if there is a loaf that they can carry, or a
message that they can send, which will carry out his plan,
they are wild to do it. So is Joanna, so is Salome yonder,
so is the other Mary, so is Martha, like their neighbors
Nathaniel and Philip, and John and Simon, and Andrew,—
they are all eager to minister to him.

Mary Magdalene stood with his mother at the cross. Mary
Magdalene saw him laid in the grave. With Salome and those
other women, Mary Magdalene went out on the Sunday of
Sundays, the first Easter Sunday of history, to enbalm his
body. And, lo! there is no body there. He is risen. It is
she whose eyes are so blinded by her tears that she does not
know him when she sees him. It is she who has only to
hear his voice, as she weeps, and she knows all. " O, my
Master ! " and the world's night is changed to everlasting
day.

From that day forward till she dies, she tells the story of
her life, her death, and her rousing to life, whenever this
child or that stranger ask her of the Master's life and love.
If they meet at his table, sometimes at Jerusalem, sometimes
at Magdala, wherever two or three meet together in his name,
if this Mary is there, there is some word of his, some story of
his, some memorial of. his gracious power and of his unwav-
ering love. Year after year passes, and at last the young
men are old men, and at last they also are all gone. All
who looked on are gone, and all who for themselves remembered. But the memorials are not gone, nor the memory of
his life and of hers. It was said of the other Mary, who
anointed his feet and wiped them with her hair,—

" Wheresoever this gospel is preached, this shall be told
as a memorial."

And of this Mary — harassed and lost as she was in earlier
days — it will always be remembered that she ministered to
her Lord, that she stood by him at the cross, and was first to
know him and to hear him at an open tomb.

[XVIII.]

C

THE

BIBLE AND ITS REVISION.

Lowe

THREE ADDRESSES

BY

Edward E. Hale.

BOSTON:

A. WILLIAMS & CO., 283 WASHINGTON STREET.

GEO. H. ELLIS, 101 MILK STREET.

1879.

GEO. H. ELLIS, PRINTER, 101 MILK STREET, BOSTON.

THE BIBLE.

Many other signs did Jesus, which are not written in this book; but these are written, that ye might believe, and that believing ye might have life in his name. If they should be written every one, I suppose that the world itself should not contain the books that should be written.
—JOHN xx., 30, 31 ; xxi., 25.

In the Bible itself there is no reference to the Bible.

There is reference to the "Book of the Law," and the Saviour once and again speaks of "the Law and the Prophets." Here he alludes to the books read in the Jewish meeting-houses of his time. Of these, all parties respected the Law as containing the historical and constitutional basis of the national existence of Israel ; while the Prophets, — including what we know as the Psalms, the Proverbs, and the book of Job, were held in varied respect by different sects. The Pharisees had also an enthusiasm of their own for the traditions, written and unwritten, which had come down to them regarding the interpretation of the Law. These, however, were only the notions of the Jews. The Christian Church, at its very birth, abridged the Jewish Law, into the mere statement that Christians must abstain from meats offered to idols, from fornication, from things strangled, and "from blood," the last cautions having special reference to the heathen sacrifice and custom of the time. And, in all the correspondences and all the legislation of the Early Church, in Christ's own words,— be it remarked especially,— there is no reference to any book, written form, written code, or scripture of any kind. Paul's phrase to a divinity student, Timothy, often quoted with a false significance, that "all scripture is given for edification," is simply an exhortation to the young man to read anything he could find. In that day of few books, he could· get good, Paul said, out of everything. It is a remark which Paul would certainly not make to-day, with regard to all the writings or publications of our time. But, considering how desirable it is that a young preacher should study, and how apt he is to prefer not to study, but to inflict his own wisdom on his

4

hearers, and how little danger there was that Timothy would
be misled in his reading, there is no wonder that Paul told
him that all that there was then in writing, Latin, Greek, or
Hebrew, was meant for edification, and would probably do
him more good than harm. The writing of books with intent to kill had not then begun.

. The Bible, then, holds the central place which it now occupies in the affection and respect of the Church of Christ,
from certain intrinsic merits of its own, which can probably
be ascertained by examination. It does not depend on any
authoritative direction of Christ, or of any of its own writers,
for acceptance and regard.

Christ, on the other hand, left the Christian Commonwealth, from age to age, under the direction of the Holy
Spirit. Each age was to find out by its best prayer and
struggle what God himself wanted it to do, and the Saviour
certified and guaranteed that each age might trust confidently to that ever-present Word. As to that criticism by
which the Jews of his time analyzed their own law, and took
away such life as it had in their vivisection, he always spoke
of that with contempt. " The letter kills, only the spirit
gives life," he says. In face of such discouragement of a
pedantic and literal interpretation of the Bible, this collection of history, prophecy, poetry, and precept, wholly unlike anything else existing, even in its literary form, holds,
by its own moral power, a central place in the Church and
in civilization. It is a place often challenged, bitterly and
fiercely; now intelligently challenged, and now stupidly.
Nay, it is a position seldom intelligently defended. The
friends of the Christian religion have said and done few
things as absurd as in their eager defence of the Bible. For
all this, however, in spite of bitter attack and in spite of
foolish defence, the Bible, of its own moral force and vitality,
holds its position. At this moment it is the book most
widely known in the world, the book most eagerly studied,
the book which exercises the most profound control over the
characters of men, and of course over the destiny of nations.
The Roman Catholic Church, in the most serious mistake of
administration which it was ever lured into, undertook, at
one period of its history, to set the weight of Bible instruction below its own, by way of giving more dignity to its own
decisions. But the Roman Church long since discovered that
error, and in our own time is as fond, I think, of citing Biblical authority or Biblical illustrations for its claims as are

the men of any communion. Certainly it has furnished, within this century, some keen and intelligent critics, both for the text and the meaning of the Bible. The Protestant Church at its birth undoubtedly fell into the counter error which has well been called Biblio-latry, — the worship of a book. This Biblio-latry found its most celebrated expression in Chillingworth's often-repeated epigram: —
. " The. Bible, and the Bible only, is the religion of Protestants."
But this epigram wholly understates the vitality or infinity of pure religion. God, in his children and in his Spirit, is the religion of Protestants, as of all Christians ; nor should any narrower statement, even in enthusiastic reverence for the Bible itself, take the place of truth so broad and simple.

The Bible holds its place, none the less, in face of the assaults of enemies, of the follies of friends, and in spite of the indifference of the careless. It holds its place, not because Christ or Paul or John appealed to it, for they did not ; not because the Church of Rome once disowned it, and afterward readopted it ; not because the Protestant Church once made it an idol ; not because the claim can be maintained that every word in it is literally or plenarily inspired. It retains its place from certain central and essential moral forces of its own, which distinguish it from other agencies acting on man or society.

It is worth while to name the more important of these in their order : —
I. First, then : the Bible is not an accidental collection, but the best result of the religious aspiration of the ages and nations in which it was formed.
The suggestion is often made in our time, that it would be an enterprise of real value to select another Bible from the religious writings of all nations,— of which it is carelessly said that there are a great many which compare not unfavorably with this Bible. But such selections are, in fact, going on all the time,— always have been going on. Literature is simply such refining and selection. The Sibylline Books of Rome were a celebrated selection of this kind. The esoteric writings of the Egyptians were a selection of this kind. Such selections always will be going on. It is popularly forgotten, I think, that the Bible itself is just such a selection. It is a selection made by exactly the law which the naturalist

6

Darwin calls the Law of Natural Selection, in which the strongest maintains its being in a struggle for life, and the weakest goes to the wall and dies. The Bible is a selection which was some two thousand years making itself, by that very law, from unnumbered prophecies, poems, precepts, histories, and letters. That which, on the test of those two thousand years, proved valuable for the eternal life of man, proved indeed invaluable,— lived. It got itself preserved in one canon or another, sifted out from chaff, and kept by the gratitude of people, who had found in it help and blessing. The little scraps of Hebrew history are mere specimen pages from volume upon volume of annals, chronicles, legends, and poems unnumbered, which have gone to their own place. The Psalms, only one hundred and fifty of them, are what were saved, century in and century out, from all the religious lyrics of the people most inclined to worship who have ever lived, whose worship involved the singing of such lyrics, and their composition, constantly. Of fifteen hundred years of such worship, there are preserved one hundred and fifty little poems, more than half of them from the inspiration of one man, the first lyric poet of all time. So of the prophecies. The orators of that people,— nay, their statesmen, their leaders of whatever kind,— uttered these eager invocations, appeals, warnings, parables, in which they illustrated God's presence and power. Of hundreds of their prophets, we have not one word. Of hundreds, nay thousands, more, we have not word nor name. Of all, we have a few fragmentary addresses by fifteen or sixteen men. Are these addresses preserved by mere accident? Not at all. They are preserved in stress of war and exile and agony,— the selected gems from other collections which had been kept in other stress of war and exile and agony,— which were what men could not part with, though in war and exile and agony, from the religious literature of warning and appeal of their country. So of the book of Job. One solitary monument of all the religious literature of a thousand years, of a race of men larger than the Hebrew race, and cultivated, as the book itself shows! From all its work of worship and religion,— the law of natural selection, thinning down and thinning down, held on to this poem, the choice and peculiar poem, which could not be lost or thrown away.

Precisely the same is true of the New Testament. Plenty of letters, of course, from Paul and other apostles. But these are those which were so well worth preserving and copying, fighting for, dying for, that these survived while the others are gone. Plenty of tales of Jesus in that first century, written here, written there. But here were four memoirs, standing test, rising above their fellows, better authenticated, more full of life.. By the law of natural selection, these live while the others die.

This is always to be remembered when people talk glibly of selections from the religious literature of all nations,— that the Bible is such a selection from selections from selections. The Old Testament is the quintessence, the fifth power, of the religious literature of the most religious race on earth ; the New Testament is the select few of the memoirs of apostolic time, which, in the early ages, survived persecution, survived scepticism, survived error and criticism, so as to maintain their own essential place as the most important memoirs of the most important event in the history of man.

II. Second. The favor with which the Bible is received by our European races, is in part the welcome they give, like a thirsty man's to water, to the Oriental habit of thought and language, which, in essence, are so much nobler and truer than our own. It is to this that we owe it, that, as Mr. Martineau says, "The Pharaohs are less strangers to our people at large than the Plantagenets, and Abraham is more distinct than Alfred."

The native habits of thought and the habits of expression of the Western or European races are of what Mr. Dickens calls the Gradgrind sort. They are apt to look at things merely in their mechanical relations. To their view, the use of the cataract is to turn a mill ; and the use of virtue is to make the house neat, and to put good things to eat on the table. Yet this is no more natural to the soul of man than it is natural to the Indian to go for two days without food. Put your new-killed venison before him, and he will show you whether his abstinence was "natural." Put your Oriental Bible, with its enthusiasm for the soul of man, for God and unseen realities, for right, truth, heaven, for beauty and loving kindness,— put this before your mechanical clodhopper of Wales or of Glasgow, of Eisenach, or of the Ober Amergau, or of New Lebanon here,— yes, or of Boston, or New York, or Chicago,— and see how it will satisfy a part of his being which none of your machinery has fed! It is to the peculiarity of race which I have indicated, that it is due, that the Bible has its most enthusiastic admirers in Western lands. The Western missionary carries it back to Persia, or even to India, and is disappointed, when, with all concession of respect for the wisdom and even truth of its contents, he cannot obtain enthusiasm for its form and language equal to that which is gained at his home. He has carried it to regions where men are used to look at the soul as substance, and not shadow ; at men and God as. the rulers of the elements, and not their slaves.

And we may safely say that God himself, in the providential training of the world, has meant that the great Eastern races should train us in faith, in the basis of all poetry, invention, and philosophy, as that we should train them in organization, in method, civil order, and the combinations of material things. We may well afford to send to them our constitutions, our manufacture, the books of our printing and the cloths of our loom, if, in the providence of God, they send us the vision of seer and the word of prophet ; teach us the syllables of our prayer and lend us the language of our hymns. It is one instance more, in God's great work, of the way in which men bear each others' burdens. It is what St. Paul, an " Easterner," speaking to "Westerners " of Rome, calls "the mutual faith of you and me." *

III. This is, however, but a local peculiarity, though a peculiarity which covers more than half the world. For the whole world the Bible asserts a distinction, which we feel, even when we do not analyze it, in the impersonality of the authors,— a characteristic not to be claimed for every line of their work, but still a dominant of the whole. There is none of the figure-posing of our modern literature, which in this resembles our modern pallet. There is none of that smirk which comes in at the balanced end of a remarkable performance, with the brazen inquiry, " Have I not done that well ?" Indeed, there is no performance at all. Solidly, very briefly, and with an intensity which has no parallel in literature, the writers drive on their purpose. " Style," the critic of other centuries talks about. But they did not worry themselves about "style." They did not know they had any style. Purpose ? Yes, they had purpose enough. To tell you and me the way in which Christ lived and died ; to tell those crazy Galatians that they were false to the whole gospel plan ; to tell Israel

* This interchange is admirably illustrated by Mr. Carlyle in his address to the students of Glasgow. .

in Babylon that, with determination and spirit, she should be free ; yes, to tell God, in his loving-kindness, that David was abject in penitence. Purpose enough, and that purpose held to, through and through,— held to with such an abandonment of the mere individualism of the writer, that we who read are always tempted to rank Matthew, Mark, Luke, and John all as one, and are almost amazed when some one compels us to notice the distinctions in the way their work is done! But the author keeps himself, almost always, behind his work.

IV. And this impersonality of the authors — their indifference to fame and to criticism — gives only more prominence to the personality, or reference to personal characteristics, which appears all through in the subjects of which they write. Half the later historical books of the Old Testament are the biography of David. The book of Acts lapses, almost by the "law of the instrument," into a biography of Paul. The Gospels make no claim but to be the biography of Christ. These are the great illustrations; and the rest are, in the same way: "Story of Abraham," "Story of Joseph," "Story of Ruth," "Story of Elijah," "Story of Deborah," "Story of Elijah and Elisha," and the rest. There is none of the ghastliness of our schools of philosophical history. There is a consciousness of the great truth that some man is behind every event in history,— that personal presence and personal power move the world. You may say, indeed, that this is only one illustration more of the necessity for which the Bible exists,— the showing that the Infinite Spirit is the Ruler of finite things. That is true. This illustration, this method in which the personality of the men and women who wrought the marvels is relied upon, is one of the ways in which that truth is forced home upon the world.

My chief effort, then, when I try to explain to young people the best way to read the Bible, is to persuade them to follow out these biographies. They do not like Paul's letters, perhaps. They will come to like them if they will study Paul's biographies, and place the letters, and make real the people to whom he writes. They make nothing of the Old Testament, perhaps. No? Let them try to make King David stand out on the canvas; let them find the costume, the scenery and circumstance, of his life; exult in his exultation when the ark entered conquered Zion, and weep in his agony when Nathan said to him, "Thou art the man." If we once rescue the Bible from that horribly blasphemous habit of reading it by chapter and verse, chopping off one piece for one day and as many inches more for the next day ; if we work out from it, now the life of a conqueror, now the life of a dreamer, now the life of a poet, and, chief of all and first of all, the living life of the Lord of Life, the Saviour of Man, it asserts for us its own moral power, and there is no need of persuasion or of authority to induce us to hold to it from that time forward.

V. For, chiefly, the Bible holds its power over men as the record, in quaint, simple, and unconscious language, of Life and the victories of Life. No literary conceit or pride of authorship, as we saw. No style, long syllables and short syllables, studied metaphor, or other critical or linguistic machinery. Rough style, indeed. You know the Roman Cardinal said he found it bad for his style, so he did not read it. Nay, no great logic ; no system of metaphysic ; no compact method of government ; no treatise on natural history ; no science of morals. Will it tell us whether there is an ocean at the North Pole ? No, it will not tell us that. Will it tell us why God permits evil ? No, it will not tell us that. Will it tell us whether the soul of man existed before he was born into this world? No. Will it tell us whether the body of man is derived in direct descent from the inferior races ? No. Then what will it tell us? It will tell us of the power of life ; of the power of God, the Life of the Universe, over all the things which he made and set in order; of the power of Man, whom God set to subdue the world, to carry out that enterprise when he loyally engages in it ; of the power of the soul, which is the life of man, to control supreme the mind of man, and his body. It tells how the spirit of God moved on the face of the waters. It tells how the inspiration of God led Israel from bondage. It tells how the sense of God lifted Israel from barbarism to command, and how, as Israel lost God, she sank back to vassalage. And such little history is accessory only to the history of histories, the centre of history ; when, in the middle of this book, four untaught men, in narration whose quaint simplicity challenges the criticism and the imitation of the world, describe some incidents in the life of God's own Son, who had no life but God's life, and obeyed no lesser law. In those fragments, there is the triumph of the great Personality of all time. Lord of Life, we call him wisely. And this race of man, which has faith in life, and can have no faith in anything else, this race,— which has always been led and which loves its leaders, which must love them and will love them,— this race of man, which despises abstractions and wants to see the truth,— this race of man, in all its doubts, selfishness, inquiry, is always glad to see the Lord of Life, to hear him speak, and to wonder, and to take to heart his victories. Because the Bible encloses the Four Gospels, explains, illustrates, leads down to them and leads back to them ; because, so leading, it shows always that life is always master, and that forms obey,— forms, methods, law, fashion, and all the outside,— that these obey and must obey ; because the Bible is the book of Life, and the book of the Lord of Life,— because of this it keeps its hold upon the world.

[This sermon with two sermons on Bible Revision are printed together, in a pamphlet of thirty-six pages, which will be found at the publishers.]

KING JAMES'S VERSION AND THE REVISION.

[An article published in *Old and New*, May, 1873, as a review of a collection of Lightfoot, Trench, and Ellicott's essays on the subject.]

The Convocation of the larger province of the Church of England has turned its serious attention to the revision of the English version of the Bible.

The curious questions which come up regarding such a revision are all, of course, at bottom, questions of criticism and literature. But questions of literature and criticism may be very central questions. The most sceptical of men, if he speaks our English language, has to recognize the power of this English Bible over that English-speaking race which rules half the world. He has to admit that this book holds the hearts of men as no other book holds them. To take Dr. Martineau's vivid expressions, " It has opened the devout and fervid East to the wonder and affection of the severer West. It has made old Egypt and Assyria more familiar to Christendom than our own lands; and to our people at large the Pharaohs are less strange than the Plantagenets, and Abraham is more distinct than Alfred. The Hebrew prophet is domesticated in the Scotch village, and is better understood when he speaks of Jordan than the poet at home when he celebrates the Greta and the Yarrow." Further yet, we may say simply, that, with all possible variations of human pride and self-reliance, still, on the whole, most men and women believe that in this book is the surest guide for life, if they can only find out what that guide says. Few men are so daring, few men rely on themselves so confidently, but they would gladly, in daily life, in any doubtful question, decide their duty by the direction of Jesus Christ, if they knew what his direction was. And, for most men, the opportunity to find that direction — that is to say, the only opportunity to find out what Jesus Christ did say and direct — is the opportunity which the Bible gives them in the language of their own country. There is no reason for wonder,

then, at the reverence, when regard is reverent, or the superstition, when it is superstitious, with which most men and
women regard this English Bible.

It is not to mere accident that the familiar English Bible
owes the hold which it has on the affections, and even on
the conscience, of half the Protestant world. King James,
whose name it bears, was, it is true, a fool; but he did two
things for which he will always be remembered,— at least in
American history. First, he drove the Pilgrim fathers out of
England, as a consequence of which we are here; and
second, in a rather melodramatic way, he ordered this translation of the Bible; and it got itself finished and published
before the new-born Protestantism of England had broken
up into sects : so that this really could become an authorized
version in general use among almost all Christians who
use the English tongue. This was a better work than could
have been expected of the man whom Mr. Haven so happily
characterizes as a "dominie spoiled into a king."

After the conference at Hampton Court, King James
selected fifty-four English scholars to do this work. Curiously little is known of the men themselves,— almost nothing. We read their words every day, careless if they were, or
who they were. In their work, however, is clear enough evidence that many of them were men of sense, and that some of
them were men of exquisite poetical sensibility and affluence
of expression. There are, for instance, no poems in the
English language which show the richness and power of that
language more marvellously, than the wonderful words with
which some unknown poet among these men has associated
the prophecies of Isaiah.

They had the wisdom, also, to use the best work of their
predecessors,— the work of men who had passed through
the fires of persecution, and at the least were true. It is a
great thing to get and to keep the martyr ring in the tone
of your Bible. More than scholarship is it, more than the
finesse of grammar, to have a Hebrew prophecy interpreted
by an English prophet, an old Jeremiad by some modern
Jeremiah, a denunciation of idolatry by a man who is fighting idolaters. That sort of "snap" and vigor came into the
English Bible from the work of Wiclif and Tyndal and Coverdale and John Rogers and other persecuted men of Queen
Mary's time; and the editors of our familiar version, though
they wrought under the patronage of a king, had the wisdom
to leave it there.

From those earlier fountains, too, came the Saxon strength
and vigor into the very language of our Bible. If we compare the fustian of the translators' preface with the unde-
filed English of the book itself, we see how glad we ought to
be that they revised the translations which they found in
existence, in preference to attempting a new one of their
own. The brother to whose pen was intrusted the dedica-
tion to the king was so left by all good angels that he
wrote : —

"Whereas it was the expectation of many who wished not
well unto our Sion, that, upon the setting of that bright Occi-
dental star, Queen Elizabeth, of most happy memory, some
thick and palpable clouds of darkness would have so over-
shadowed this land that men should have been in doubt
which way they were to walk," and much more in the same
high-wrought strain. To compare that bombast in mere language with the work of the pen that wrote, " King Agrippa,
believest thou the prophets ? I know that thou believest,"
or with the work of the pen that wrote, " Nathan said unto
David, Thou art the man,"— is to see why we are to be
grateful to the Providence that gives us the Saxon of Wiclif
for our religious reading, instead of the euphuistic flummery
of a courtier of King James.

Wholly apart, also, from any measure of its divine inspiration, the English Bible has a worth which we cannot fully
state, as the monument which commemorates, and the talisman which preserves, the English language. It is the best
memorial of that language as it existed in its very best time.
And because it is read in every cottage, and quoted in every
workshop and on every exchange, it preserves the English
language, and keeps it from wandering far from its originals.
In Mr. Marsh's beautiful figure, it is the central sun around
which the English language revolves in its orbit; and, in
point of fact, the English spoken to-day is even nearer the
English of the English Bible than was that written by Addi-
son, by Dr. Johnson, and by Cotton Mather. The centrip-
etal attraction governs ; and from this sacred centre the
language cannot wander far. We must recognize the same
Providence in the sister fact, not so important, but not to be
forgotten, that the English of that very period is the English
of Shakspeare,— the only poet who holds sway over all
speakers of the English tongue in all time,— the man whose
wisdom is quoted, and whose wit is remembered, in cottage
and in palace, and will be. His hold on the heart of Eng-

lishmen, and the descendants of Englishmen, is one bond
more — and that no weak one — to hold them firm and faithful to the familiar use of the English of the English Bible.
Thus,—

> " To outweigh all harm, the sacred book,
> In dusty sequestration wrapped too long,
> Assumes the accents of our native tongue ;
> And he who guides the plough, or wields the crook,
> With understanding spirit now may look
> Upon her records, listen to her song,
> And sift her laws, much wondering that the wrong
> Which faith hath suffered Heaven could calmly brook." *

To American readers, it may be a convenient help to
memory to recollect that this version was published after the
Pilgrim fathers left England for Holland, before they left
Holland for New England. In point of fact, therefore, they
used and cited the older versions, as did the early Virgin-
ians ; while Winthrop's company, landing in "the Bay," in
1630, brought with them, and used King James's version.
Of course, this distinction was obliterated long ago. King
James's version, so-called, was first published in 1613. It is
always called "The Authorized Version," or "King James's
Version." It proves, however, that it was never, in form,
authorized by any authority, excepting that the king originally named the fifty-four scholars who prepared it. After it
was made, the king's printers and the universities had the
privilege of printing it; and as it was, unquestionably, the
best version made up to that time, it worked its way into
general use, and is at this moment The Bible, as the Bible is
practically known to people using the English tongue. This
is the Bible which it is now proposed, by a far more general
assent than could have been thought possible, to revise.

The proposal comes from a body, the most respectable for
numbers represented, and the most conservative in opinion,
in the Protestant Church,— from the body known as "The
Convocation of the Province of Canterbury of the Church
of England."

Since the time of Edward I., the clergy of the two provinces of the Church of England — Canterbury and York —
have had the right of meeting in a sort of parliament of
their own, called a Convocation. Till Charles II.'s time,
they voted their own taxes; and the clergy did not pay taxes
as civilians did. Since that time, the meeting of Convoca-

* Wordsworth.

tion has been ornamental merely; it was called together, indeed, only for form, for more than a century. But with the resurrection of the Church of England, which this generation has witnessed, the meetings of Convocation have assumed more interest.

There are men in the Church of England, as there are in all churches, who would gladly give the whole government, and, indeed, all interests of the Church, to the clergy alone. That is the bane and ruin of the Roman Church. Practically its clergy is "the Church." Such men would gladly gain for "Convocation" the government of the English Church, and are hoping and praying that it may gain it.

But the government of England, and the wisest men in the Church of England, have no such idea. They know that the church of a land embodies all the Christianity in a land, though, as a part of that Christianity, there must be included the poor hope for forgiveness of a felon waiting death in prison. They therefore give the government of the Church to the people of the land, and to no elect class among that people, muttering, "We are holier than you." At whatever moment, therefore, "Convocation" begins to interfere in the government of the Church of England, a message from the real government of England invariably dismisses "Convocation."

None the less is it evident, that a meeting of nearly all the bishops of England, and of representatives chosen by its clergy, must be a distinguished and learned body; and when this body, at its meeting in February, 1870, proposed a revision of the English Bible, the proposal commanded very general respect. The "Convocation" undoubtedly represented the largest body of Protestant people speaking our language,— perhaps speaking any language. And, with a freedom worthy of this century, it proposed that the committee intrusted with the work of revision should be at liberty to "invite the coöperation of any persons eminent for scholarship, to whatever nation or religious body they may belong."

On this vote, a very strong committee was appointed; and this committee have sought and obtained the help of distinguished scholars in every religious body both in England and America. The committees have adopted a judicious plan of work, and are diligently engaged in the revision.

We are certain that, to the average Christian man or

woman, nothing can be more distasteful than the idea of pulling the Bible to pieces to improve upon it. Let us have the "thees" and "thous," people say. Let us have the quaintness and simplicity. Do let us hear the Bible read as we heard it when we were children. To this cry, in substance, we certainly say, "Amen"; and it is a satisfaction to say that the Board of Revision says so. They are a board of revision, not of translation. They mean simply to take errors out of the text, and compel the English language, if they can, to say all that the Greek and Hebrew do; but they mean that the Bible shall speak in the language it speaks in now, with no modern innovation, and, in general, "to introduce as few alterations as are consistent with faithfulness." They have undertaken, for instance, if possible, to use no word not now used in the English version, or one of the earlier versions.

Now we may say, very briefly, that there is no doubt,— 1. That the Greek text of the New Testament is now much more accurately known than it was in King James's time. To allude to recent improvements, which readers who do not profess to be critics will understand, but which are by no means the most important which we could cite, it is within fifteen years that, as a moral consequence of the revolution in Italy, the Pope has thrown open to the free use of critics the celebrated Vatican manuscript, long thought to be the oldest in existence. As late as the year 1859, Constantine Tischendorf discovered in the Convent of Mt. Sinai the manuscript known as Aleph,— the oldest manuscript of the Bible known. A greater advantage than either of these, perhaps, is the facility given by photographic copies of ancient manuscripts to the scholars of all countries to use the treasures of libraries to which they cannot travel. From such sources, and from the tireless labor of a new school of critics determined to remove inaccuracy from the text, we have now substantially the language of the books of the New Testament as they were written, with very little room for question on matters of importance.

2. In the second place, the best scholars of to-day know Greek and Hebrew much better than did the scholars of King James's time ; and,—

3. Three centuries of stiff study and controversy have thrown no little light on the illustration given from one part of Scripture to another, and given from other literature to Scripture literature.

There is no doubt, therefore, that a loyal desire to have
the truth, the whole truth, and nothing but the truth will
compel Christians who speak English to consent to a revision
of the authorized version. Strange to say, it is not the extreme liberals, the purists of the Puritans, who care most for
it. We have long got beyond Chillingworth's narrow motto,
which was, "The Bible, and the Bible only, is the religion of
Protestants." We have come so far as to say, "God, and
God only, gives the religion to Christians"; and we believe
that God has a thousand voices which are to be studied, as
well as the directions of the Scripture. But none the less,
as we have said, the Bible, if not the only authority, is the
leading authority, with all Christian men; and in mere
decency, in common honesty, nay, in loyalty to truth, they
must read what its writers really said, with no man's gloss
upon it, or emasculations.

And, in this whole business, the grand thing is the honest
desire for the truth, observable in all the leaders. It is no
longer a petty hope that "our side" may triumph. There is
the certainty that "our side" cannot triumph, and that no
side can triumph, unless the truth triumphs. Protestantism
may have failed in other duties of organized religion; it
may not find out the lowest and vilest of men and women in
their dens; it may not reconcile classes of society to each
other; it may not be successful in its arrangements for
ritual: but it has come so far, that its real leaders in every
party live and die for the truth, let the truth say what it will
about their old histories or their conflicts. A noble illustration of this is the loyalty with which all the scholars who
have as yet published their views as to this revision have
surrendered the three great Trinitarian proof-texts. They
acknowledge that they are all spurious additions of a late
date to the record, and must go.

1. "There are three that bear witness in heaven." —
I. JOHN.

2. "God was . . . received up into glory."— I. TIM. iii., 16.

3. "The Church of God, which he hath purchased with his
own blood." — ACTS xx., 28.

These gentlemen — all of them Trinitarians, who would
be very glad to believe that these texts were genuine — manfully disown them. They are not genuine; and these men
will not fight for victory under false colors. Such willing-
ness of the Church to unite for the truth is worth more than
all the corrections put together which they will introduce
into the familiar text of Scripture.

In such a paper as this, it is, of course, impossible to go into the detail which alone gives the charm to the book which we have mentioned. It is hard to say which of the three treatises included in it have the most interest for an intelligent reader. We must be satisfied with saying that nine-tenths of the stumbling-blocks, little or great, will drop out of the Bible in the revision. There are obscure passages, which people do not understand, find it hard to believe, and hate, if they would only say so. Intelligent clergymen, in reading from the pulpit, lighten such passages as they read. Every reader has the right to such enlightenment, if it can be given him.

"Men of Athens," said Paul, "I perceive that in all things you are greatly inclined to worship." He never insulted them by saying, "You are too superstitious."

"Be not anxious for your life, what ye shall eat, or what shall you drink." This is what Jesus said, always the most practical of teachers. He never said what we mean when we say, "Take no thought for your life, what ye shall eat, or what ye shall drink."

"If Jesus had given men rest, David would not have spoken of another day," says the Epistle to the Hebrews. It should read, "if *Joshua* had given them rest"; and till it does, is unintelligible.

There are hundreds of cases where the change of use in a preposition or adverb makes the sense dark, where, to an ordinary reader of the Greek, it is perfectly simple. "By and by he is offended," now means, "he will be offended in the future": in King James's time, it invariably meant, "is offended now."

The "beasts in heaven" will disappear from the Revelations. They are "living creatures," so glorious that the poet could give them no name but the name of "the living."

"Eateth and drinketh damnation," will disappear.

The fifth chapter of Romans will become intelligible and credible.

The truth will appear as to the government of the early churches, so far as they had any.

These are only instances out of hundreds; for in hundreds of such passages will the New Testament, at least, become easier to understand.

But a change more important will be in a slight increase in that marvellous freshness which is even now the glory of the English Bible. Where the old translators did not know the meaning, they could not express it; and they blurred it, or slurred it, as ingenious children at school do in translating what they do not understand. Then, too, King James's revisers were not free, as has been said, from a notion of mock elegance of expression, borrowed from the Euphues of their time, which just at this moment, when firm Saxon is the fashion, we have outgrown.

But, after all, the change is homage to the truth. It is a change due to the conviction of our time that there are no trifles; that we will have the truth in art, in science, in literature, in conversation, even in the setting of a play on the stage, or we will have nothing. The change will in no way materially affect the visible currents of Christian life. There is many an intelligent congregation, to whom a dozen verses of Bishop Ellicott's specimen of the probable revision could be read, without the knowledge of one hearer in a hundred that the familiar text was changed. And, so far as dogma goes, the dogmatic controversialists have long since gone behind one version or another, to fight, each for his own, from the text of the original. We shall not gain any material improvement in dogma by this revision. We shall gain two other things; and they are great things:—

1. Even in this sedulous care to bring the Scripture to its purity, the idolatry of the letter is gone forever. Men do not scrape and file and polish the idol which they worship; they take it in all its ugliness,—" the stone which fell from heaven," the figure-head of the old wreck as it was washed ashore: but they take it as it is, and they do not pretend to refine upon it. The moment when the Christian Church solidly and squarely sets itself to work on a task like this, reason is enthroned, and superstition dies. Grant to a hundred of the purest and wisest men in England and America the right to determine which reading shall be selected, and which version used, and you have restored the Bible to its true place. It is the human record of the most extraordinary events in history. It is no longer a stupid oracle, with a " Thus saith the Lord," speaking imperatively for contingencies and difficulties never dreamed of when it was written. It becomes the intelligible and living statement of what has happened in ages of faith, among men who believed in God, when they obeyed, and when they disobeyed. To restore the Bible thus to its true position, to begin to worship God again, and to turn to God again, and to seek his Holy Spirit, and to turn away from that idolatry

of a book which, for two centuries, fettered half Christendom,— this is a victory, and a great victory.

2. And the second victory of the revision is no less. In this homage to the truth, practically all Christians are uniting. To see Wilberforce the High-Churchman, Stanley broadest of the broad, Vance Smith the Unitarian, Geden the Methodist, Davies the Baptist, Roberts the Presbyterian, with a hundred others of every name that can be named, kneeling together in Westminster Abbey to receive the symbols of the Christian communion before they entered upon this duty,— that was a sight which Cranmer, Latimer, Tyndal, and Coverdale had never seen before,— no, not since they were translated. It may well have given new joy to the heaven which is their home. Behind the clamor of party, behind the method of administration, behind the incense of ritual and the adjustment of liturgy, appears now the determination that we will come together, and work together ; for each other we will live as for each other these martyrs died, in the love of God, in drawing nearer to God in the discovery of the truth, and in homage to the truth. To show that this is the central desire of all sects is the crowning victory of this experiment, in itself so little. It shows what is the common ground on which we all are standing. In that common accord the Church is indeed made sacred. " Sanctify them through Thy truth: thy word is truth."

THE REVISION OF THE BIBLE.

The righteousness which is of faith speaketh on this wise:
"The word is nigh thee, in thy mouth and in·thy heart; that is, the
word of faith which we preach."— ROMANS x., 6–8.

Nine years ago, in February, 1870, the Convocation of
Canterbury, which represents the largest part of the Church
of England, proposed a revision of the Bible, as it is read in
churches, in all English-speaking lands. In September, 1870,
the work in England began. A part of the plan proposed
that a body of scholars in America should carry on the work
contemporaneously with the English Commission. Such a
board was appointed and began its work in 1872. I remember speaking here of the enterprise soon after, and trying to
show what was the class of difficulties in Scripture reading
which it might be hoped it would remove. What I said then
I printed at the time, and I do not return to that subject
now; for the work is so nearly done that we may soon test
the fruits for ourselves. Let me try to tell you briefly what
has been done by way of preparation for the day, not very
distant, when I shall be reading here from a Bible more
accurate than I have ever read from here before.

The American Commission made what I may call its
report of progress at a large meeting held in this city on
Thursday last. The meeting was itself a historic occasion.
From distant parts of the country had come together these
scholars, whose skill in the languages has given them the
distinguished privilege of weighing again the words which,
in an English tongue, shall represent the old Hebrew and
Chaldee and Greek. To meet them had been summoned
presidents and professors in colleges, a large number of the
clergy of all communions, and of distinguished gentlemen in
other callings, all interested in knowing what is to be this
rendering of those Scriptures, on which, in so large measure,
depend our written laws, and so much of our religious and
social order. Seven of the gentlemen concerned in the work

of revision explained the method and object of that work, in addresses made to this assembly; and then, by spokesmen of authority, the meeting expressed its profound interest in the undertaking. This interest was expressed in other ways indeed, and there can be no doubt that the best scholarship and thought of the United States and of England are in sympathy with this endeavor to improve the popular knowledge of the Scriptures.

At this meeting it was announced that the work of the English Commission on the New Testament is in substance finished. It only awaits the incorporation of the suggestions of the American Commission on some of Paul's Epistles. It would perhaps be possible to print it within a year, unless its publication be deferred to the completion of the Old Testament. The Old Testament work is the more slow, and there is more of it. It will not be finished probably for two years. There are some reasons for deferring the publication of the New Testament to the completion of the Old. It would be well, for instance, if, in the citation of a psalm or a prophecy in the New Testament, the words should be the same in both parts of the Bible. This is not so, as the Bible stands, and, of course, a certain inconvenience follows.

I. The enterprise in hand is not a new translation of the Bible into the language of to-day. That Divine Law which men now call "natural selection," and now " Providence," has so ordered history that the English Bible is the noblest monument of the English language. It was translated by martyrs, men who took their lives in their hands that they might translate it. That gave movement and energy to its words of Infinite Life. It took its present form in the young, exuberant life of the English language, when, as has been well said, men were using the language with the joy of discoverers,— in the time which made immortal Spenser, and Sidney, and Bacon, and Shakspeare. Our timid days, our life in the purple or the palace, our critical weighing of words, will never give us the flow of language or the power of speech which men had then. We know too well to think that we can write better prose than Bacon, better poetry than Shakspeare, or clothe Isaiah in words more divine than some unknown poet chose for Isaiah in this book, or write narrative more pure than that in which Wiclif and Tyndale and Coverdale clothed Matthew's Gospel. The translation, in its form and dialect, is to be retained. Even the method of language, though it seem quaint, is to be preserved in any corrections. No word is to be used in it not in our Bible now. What we make is, not a new translation, but a revision of that we had before. We retain the "thees" and the "thous." We retain the Saxon conciseness and quaintness. We retain "Thus saith the Lord." We retain every syllable of the Lord's Prayer, and, I think, every word of the Ten Commandments. I once tried the experiment of reading here ten or twelve verses of the New Testament in Bishop Ellicott's specimen of the revision. The passage was not a specially familiar one, though not unfamiliar. I think no person in this congregation knew of the change till I told them; so that no sensibilities need be shocked as to the degree or bad taste of the proposed alteration.

It is by revision, indeed, not by new translation, that the English Bible became what it is. The first work, practically, was by Wiclif, more than a hundred years before Columbus discovered America. Decade by decade, generation by generation, men improved on his version. The fatal idea of a finished or even an authorized version did not exist in those times. The art of printing gave new zeal to translators. The Reformation quickened them to passionate enthusiasm. They learned Hebrew and Greek more carefully, that they might better render the Scripture. And, as I have said, their own language was taking on the perfect symmetry and the exquisite beauty of its maiden youth. From the time of Wiclif, in 1380, till King James's version, as we call it, was printed in 1611,— a period of more than two centuries,— this process of correction went steadily on. With every generation, the danger of mistake to the English reader was diminished,—

"Fine. by degrees. and beautifully less."

In certain minor matters, indeed, this revision has gone forward ever since. The proof-readers, or correctors of the press, have taken liberties which no law ·permitted, but common-sense has justified. Obsolete words have given place to modern spelling under their eye. Thus, "moe" becomes "more," "causey" becomes "causeway," "aliant" becomes "alien," he "neesed" becomes he "sneezed," at the simple discretion of the printers. But such discretion varies; so that, in another place, you may find the obsolete word unchanged. The first edition of King James substituted the black word Judas for the loved name of Jesus, in one unfortunate passage. The error was corrected in the next, but no like authority has been sufficient to correct other errors as gross, till now.

II. Failing any authority for gradual correction, there has accumulated, in two and a half centuries of human progress, much knowledge on the Scripture which ought to be incorporated in the people's Bible, but is still shut up as the peculiar possession of scholars.

1. We know the text of the New Testament much better than men knew it in the seventeenth century. The translators of King James's time used a Greek Testament printed by Erasmus. We know now that this was based on manuscripts comparatively late and not very accurate. The worst story of its inaccuracy is in the fact that there is one passage where Erasmus himself wrote the Greek,— the last six verses of the Revelations,— translating them from the Latin back to Greek, because they were lost from his manuscript. Perhaps from mere convenience to the printer, he made the basis of his work one of the latest manuscripts he had, belonging to the sixteenth century. In place of this,— for a single instance of our many resources,— we can now compare twenty-six uncial manuscripts, as they are called, running from the fourth century to the tenth, of which Erasmus never saw but one, and that one he did not use. We have the diligent and almost fanatical study which the same centuries have given to the ancient versions into other languages, and to the quotations made by the earliest fathers of the Church. We are thus able to speak with a very near approach to substantial certainty, not literal precision, as to the words written by Paul, Luke, Mark, and the rest. I should say that there is not left a single important passage where scholars have any real doubt as to the drift of the language first employed. Of course the variation in detail is endless; but so great was the care always taken by copyists, that these variations do not often strike at very critical or important subjects of discussion.*

2. I have been speaking of the Greek text of the New Testament. Within narrower limits, I may say that we have also a somewhat better Hebrew text of the Old Testament than the translators of King James had. What is much more

* I append at the close of this sermon an illustration of this statement from the Sermon on the Mount.

important, men know Hebrew vastly better than they knew it
then. They had then only such a knowledge as the Jews of
their time had, such a knowledge as a man brings home of
the conversational language of a country he has travelled in.
Men have now a careful scientific knowledge of Hebrew.
They have studied it in its relations with Arabic, with which
it is almost as closely connected as is Italian with Latin, and
in its relations with other languages of the same family.
Now the translators of King James's time knew Greek very
well. We have, therefore, a good Greek translation of a
careless text of the New Testament. But the men who translated the Old Testament did not know Hebrew very well.
We have, therefore, in King James's Bible, not a very good
translation of what was quite a good text of the Old Testament. The revision will show, for these reasons, many
more important changes in the language of the Old Testament than in that of the New.

III. Next to this fundamental matter — what shall they
translate — comes the question, "Who shall translate, or
who shall revise?"

This matter has been admirably well arranged, with much
more ease than could have been thought possible. The Convocation of Canterbury represents the largest section of the
English Church,— a sort of conference of the clergy, without
political power, but with great moral and advisory power,
when it has a chance to act. In February, 1870, this Convocation proposed the new revision, and, loyal to truth, rising
quite above lines of sect, proposed it should be entrusted to
scholars of every communion. It was afterwards arranged
that a body of American scholars should make an auxiliary
commission, to work, on this side of the water, side by side
with the Commission in England, and that the two Commissions should interchange results, acting on the same general
plan. This broad scheme has been happily carried out.
Every leading branch of the English-speaking Church is represented.* The English Commission consists of fifty-two
scholars ; the American,— which was named on our side,
by representative men and scholars,— of twenty-six. The
reputations of men of classical and Hebrew scholarship do
not generally travel far outside the circle of their immediate
readers ; but in this company are some names well known

* Our own communion, by Mr. Vance Smith. in England, and Professor Abbot, here.
Nor could we ask for representatives more creditable.

in general literature. Such are the names, in Great Britain, of Alford and Wilberforce, no longer living ; of Dean Stanley, Archbishop Trench, Dr. Wordsworth, and Bishops Ellicott and Lightfoot. With us, the names of Dr. Schaff, of Dr. Stowe, of Dr. Warren, Professor Abbot, and Dr. Thayer will be generally known. The only danger in such a selection is, that the mood of the scholar, with its sharp, hard accuracy, may be too much for the stress and life of the poet, always more true, though less angular. Now the Bible is preëminently a book of poetry, and it always has proved, in this world, that the insight of the poet is worth more for truth than the precision of the rabbi. To have made either Commission quite perfect, the British Commission should have remembered the value of good English as well as good Hebrew, and given seats to Tennyson and Gladstone, as we might do to Bryant and Longfellow. But, in a revision which owes so much to Dr. Stanley's care, everything is to be hoped ; and, though it early lost Dr. Alford, it is known that his spirit guided the selection of his associates.

IV. This is not the place for a description of the method of work. The two Commissions, separated by the ocean, have worked independently, each in two companies,— an Old Testament and a New Testament company,— and have exchanged, confidentially, in print, their results. A little incident, narrated on Thursday, shows how thorough is the work on each side. It so happened that the two Commissions exchanged their first drafts of the Epistle to the Hebrews, each sending its note without having seen the other's. When the English text arrived here, it proved that the Commission had made nine hundred and thirteen changes in our present version. Of these, four hundred and seventy-six had been already suggested in the same identical words, by their American brethren, without concert with them. A similar coincidence was observed by the Old Testament companies, when they exchanged, in the same way, the prophecy of Isaiah.

Under such auspices, it is now announced that the New Testament is in substance completed, after a constant work of ten years. It only needs the last work of the American revisers, and the consideration of their criticisms in England. It may be that the New Testament may be printed so that we may use it in this pulpit in another year. The Old Testament, from its length, and from intrinsic difficulties, requires ·re time. Two years more will be requisite to complete it.

When finished, the new revision will not be introduced by any authority. The days of such authority are over. Even our present Bible was never introduced by authority. The translators were appointed by King James; they did their work, and the universities printed it. That was all. It was the best English Bible, and in time people bought it. But if it were not the best, it would not be used. If it were not the best to-day, it would not be read from this pulpit; and when a better best comes, that better best will take its place, not by any leap, not by any command, but as any new edition takes the place of an older edition,— as men read Bryant's *Iliad* more than they read Chapman's, even though there are many lines better in Chapman than there are in Bryant. The Earl of Shaftesbury, in a foolish attack on the revision, said that it was an effort by synodical interference to destroy all the existing Bibles in the world. I might as well say that the Waltham Watch Company was an effort by corporate interference to destroy all the existing watches in the world. If the Waltham watch prove the best, careful people will carry it. Gradually old watches will wear out, and then those who use them will buy new ones. But watch or Bible will be known by its fruits. There is no other test in earth; no, nor in heaven!

I have no hesitation in prophesying that, in a generation, the revised Bible will be in ninety-nine out of a hundred of the pulpits of English-speaking Christendom. I have none in saying that it will be in this pulpit the day that it can first be brought to Boston, if I am that day the servant of this church,— as I hope to be. "That more light and more truth are coming out of God's Holy Word,"— by that prophecy John Robinson consecrated New England the day of her birth and baptism. "More light and more truth,"— to that prophecy New England has held up the country, forced it up, when necessary, in the crash of battle and by the arbitrament of war. "To more light and more truth," is all our liberal Christian movement pledged. And this church would cease to be, if she ceased to proclaim the same word of promise.

"From God's Holy Word, more light, more truth, and more!"

V. At the same time, it is true that we have not the same sort of interest in this great enterprise which our friends of other communions feel. We have learned what they seem have yet to learn, that "the letter killeth and only the spirit giveth life." If the spirit of man is true enough and wise enough and has light enough from God to sit in judgment on two texts in two parchments, and decide which of them is better than the other, then is it true that the "spirit of man is the candle of the Lord." Our fathers have bravely gone through this business of analyzing the written word, and finding the value of its jots and of its tittles. We have entered into their work, and ought to be grateful to them, that they have done it for us so well as they have. To us the "Word of God" is what it was to St. John,—every expression of God's will and his power. To us it is true that he smiles in the sunbeam, it is true that he speaks in the tempest, it is true that his handwriting is over all the world. "He never left himself without a witness in that he did good." Of his dealings with Israel in her days of idolatry and weakness, we are glad to have Israel's record. Of his revelation of himself in Jesus Christ, we are glad to have the record made by Christ's disciples. But, in either case, these are the records of a revelation and not the revelation itself. And while we are adjusting and readjusting words and phrases, we can never impudently assert for our own work, when it is done, that this is a faultless and unique oracle of the Word of God!

Nor do I make this proud claim for our handful of churches only. We must look on this whole enterprise of revision as a final death-blow to that idolatry of the Bible, in all Protestant churches, which paralyzed the first triumphs of the Reformation, and has so benumbed religion for these later centuries. In the midst of the first true enthusiasm of "justification by faith," men were stopped by their leaders, as if they were told that God had forgotten his world, that he had gone on a journey, like Baal, and had left behind him a finished book, as his last will and testament for mankind. This book they were to worship as if it had been a stone which fell from heaven. That worship of word and letter has benumbed Christendom while it lasted. For there cannot be the pure religion of the Spirit, when men are bending all their energy to construe the enigmas of an oracle. Of that idolatry, I say the end has come now. For men do not take their idol from its shrine, and polish it, and clean it, insert a new jewel in this eye, and trim down the fold of that lock of hair, if they mean to fall down and worship it when once more it stands upon the pedestal. In the course of the discussions of the revision, I have heard one learned man of an evangelical school say, with charming simplicity, that he supposed all his hearers knew that it was only the consonants of the Old Testament Hebrew which were directed by the inspiration of God, but that the vowels, appended to these consonants, are simply the uninspired work of man. When we come to as fine a point as that,—inspired consonants and uninspired vowels,—the whole idolatry of the letter is of course tumbling to its fall. After eighteen centuries the indignant protest of Jesus Christ against the worship of the letter will begin to have its sway, and will really enter into the understandings of men.

From this time forth, as I believe, we may look for another advance — slow but sure — of the religion of life. To know that people and preacher have one Bible, is a help to that religion. The secrets which learned men have known about this book are henceforth to be the property of him that runs. So much is gained. More than this, the mock mystery surrounding it is over. Men will read it for what it is. Better than this, and more, it will be help and not hindrance. The noblest voice of the ages to the children of God, it will speak to them now to assert their relationship to him, to bid them listen to all his voices, and to enter into his work. "Where two or three are gathered together in my name, there am I in the midst of them." "I will send you another comforter, who shall abide with you forever." "The Word is nigh thee, in thy heart and in thy mouth." "Why not of your own selves judge ye what is right?" These are the promises, the encouragements, the directions. And man, the Son of God as he is, life from God's life, inspired by his Spirit, will use every word spoken here to the fathers; will use every word written yonder in the sunbeam or on the snow-flake; will hearken as well to every whisper of his own true heart; and will interpret every oracle spoken in the Gentile history of mankind. The Word of God shall have full course. The leaf shall be for fruit and the root for medicine. And so, with every day of every year, shall man come nearer to God.

So, with every day of every year, shall God's kingdom come!

THE PROBABLE REVISION.

To illustrate the similarity between the approved text and
that to which we are accustomed, I read the following passage
from Bishop Ellicott's statement of the probable results of
revision. It will be observed that it differs from the English
of our Bibles in only three passages.

"And seeing the multitudes he went up into the mountain,
and when he was set, his disciples came unto him. And he
opened his mouth and taught them, saying, —

"Blessed *are* the poor in spirit: for theirs is the kingdom
of heaven. Blessed *are* they that mourn: for they shall be
comforted. Blessed *are* the meek: for they shall inherit the
earth. Blessed *are* they that hunger and thirst after righteousness: for they shall be filled. Blessed *are* the merciful:
for they shall obtain mercy. Blessed *are* the pure in heart:
for they shall see God. Blessed *are* the peacemakers: for
they shall be called the sons of God. Blessed are they which
are persecuted for righteousness' sake: for theirs is the kingdom of heaven. Blessed are ye when men shall revile you,
and persecute you, and shall say all manner of evil against
you falsely, for my sake. Rejoice and be exceeding glad, for
great is your reward in heaven: for so persecuted they the
prophets which were before you."

I do not mean to say that these three variations fairly
illustrate the importance of the variations which will be made
by the revision. I cited this passage rather for the purpose
of showing that the most familiar passages of the Testament
are, by a very natural law, those in which the least variation
is made by copyists.

No person is yet at liberty to state publicly what are the
results of the commission. But Bishop Ellicott, whose authority is very high, has given this illustration of the "probable revision."

THE

FUTURE OF NEW ENGLAND.

A SERMON

PREACHED IN THE SOUTH CONGREGATIONAL CHURCH,
BOSTON,

FAST DAY, APRIL 3, 1879.

BY

EDWARD E. HALE.

BOSTON:

A. WILLIAMS & CO., 283 WASHINGTON STREET.
GEO. H. ELLIS, 101 MILK STREET.

1879.

FROM THANKSGIVING TO FAST.

The following sermons have been printed in this series : —

THE GREAT HARVEST YEAR,

LOOKING BACK,

RITUAL,

PRAYER,

RESPECTABILITY,

YOURSELVES,

WHAT IT IS TO BE CATHOLIC,

THE JOY OF LIFE,

THE ASSOCIATED CHARITIES,

THE REVISION OF THE BIBLE,

THE BIBLE,

LENT,

NEW LIFE,

BLASPHEMY AGAINST THE HOLY GHOST,

THE FUTURE OF NEW ENGLAND.

The whole series, neatly bound, may be bought from the Publishers, or from R. B. Palfrey, 12 Garland Street.

Price, $1.00 in paper, $1.25 in cloth.

THE FUTURE OF NEW ENGLAND.

In speaking of the future of New England, I am following
in the steps of Dr. Ezra Stiles, as he addressed a conven-
tion on the same subject, one hundred and nineteen years
ago. He was one of the most careful scholars of New England in the period just before the American Revolution.
His studies on various subjects are well worth our attention
now; and of all his published works, none is more interesting than his discourse "On the Christian Union," delivered
in Bristol, Rhode Island, April 23, 1760.

In this discourse, he goes into very careful statistics, to
show what will be the probable increase of New England,
first in the next century, and then in several hundred years
after, till the millennium. Without following the detail, which
shows care and judgment unusual among men who forecast
the future, I will say simply that his prophecy is, that in the
year 1860 the population of Connecticut, Rhode Island, and
Massachusetts would be about eight millions of people. He
makes allowance for the considerable settlement of Vermont; he takes notice of the fact that Nova Scotia is already
receiving settlers from New England; and with a certain generosity, quite striking in the praise of his own home, he
says: "If Providence shall complete the reduction of
Canada and an honorable peace to the British Crown, we
may extend our settlements to new provinces, or to the
western parts of those provinces which, by their charters,
cross the continent to the Pacific Ocean." But he does not
anticipate any such settlement on a very large scale. He
says "the present bounds of New England, the greater part
of which is a wilderness, permit an increase of seven millions"; and he bestows a good deal of care on an argument
which shows why the New Englander will not settle in New
York, New Jersey, or in Pennsylvania. He closes this preface by transporting his hearers to the distance of one hundred years forward from the time in which he speaks. He
asks them to look over this wide-spread wilderness of New
England, "to see it blossom like the rose, and behold it

4

planted with churches and temples consecrate to the *pure worship* of the Most High,—when our present plain edifices for public worship shall be succeeded with a nobler species of building, not, indeed, with temples whose colonnades are decked with the gilt busts of angels winged, but temples adorned with all the decent ornaments of the most sublime and august architecture; when divinely resplendent truth shall triumph, and our brethren of the Congregational communion may form a body of SEVEN MILLIONS! A glorious and respectable body this, for TRUTH and LIBERTY! Well might our fathers die with pleasure, and sacrifice their lives with joy, to lay the foundation of such a name, of such a peculiar people, whose numbers so soon increase as the sand of the sea or the stars of heaven, and, what is more, whose God is the Lord."

These sanguine hopes of one of the most far-sighted men who has ever lived in New England were doomed, so far as her population goes, to be disappointed. Far-sighted men will overlook something. In this case, the mathematics of Dr. Stiles did not deceive him. It has proved, indeed, that his figures were curiously correct. What he could not believe was, that any New Englander should ever willingly leave New England. Least of all did Dr. Stiles conceive it possible that many men should go beyond the country of the savage Six Nations, even beyond the "Alleghany Mountain," as Dr. Stiles would have called that range, even beyond the "great river of the West," of which he knew so little, nay even beyond the mountains beyond that river, nay even to the great Southern Sea. With us, the typical New Englander is the man who looks in on everything between pole and pole. But this habit had not shown itself then. The New Englander was still a fisherman and navigator, but he had shown no disposition for distant explorations of the interior. It is true that there is a single tradition, which is probably true, that the men of Massachusetts anticipated La Salle in his discovery of the Mississippi, and that the Indians who led him on this discovery had learned their way under the direction of Massachusetts adventurers. But in the very fact that we cannot wear this laurel, because nobody followed up their discovery, in the fact that for three-quarters of a century France and her Jesuits were left to have their own way in that great valley, is an illustration of the indisposition of our people in general toward inland adventure.

It was not till the Revolutionary War was over that that change came over New England which has resulted in the complete falsification of Ezra Stiles's prophecies. The two wars had given to the new nation the eastern side of the Valley of the Mississippi, as far south as the northern line of Florida. Officers and soldiers who had been discharged from the army found nothing to do at home in the terrible prostration of all trade. Congress was glad enough to pay off its debts to them by grants of land which seem enormous even to our views of land subsidies. Four years after the peace, Manasseh Cutler, a Connecticut minister, led the first colony to Ohio. He covered his emigrant wagon with black canvas on which he painted the words, "Ohio: for Marietta on the Muskingum."

This wagon was the "Mayflower " of the North-west. She started on her voyage only ninety-two years ago. Forty-five men went out with Cutler. You know how the New Englanders have followed their example. That day, they broke their bounds. They passed beyond the Six Nations ; they crossed the head waters of the Ohio ; they began on that system of penetration of every corner of every valley in this continent, which at this moment gives you a graduate of Harvard College for your host, though you be botanizing in Alaska, or hangs a picture of the Charter Oak over your head as you lie in bed in a cabin in Colorado.

There is no doubt that the leaders of New England at home looked with anxiety on this westward drift. The bitter aversion to the acquisition of Louisiana by the United States was due, in part at least, to such anxiety. When my father was in college, the Philotechnic Society, to which he belonged, discussed in 1803 the question, " Whether the acquisition of Louisiana would be an advantage to the United States? Decided in the negative." I think the vote was 34 to 5. In a pamphlet published in 1804, the writer uses the following language : ... "The settlement of our new lands will be discouraged by allurements to regions of greater promise and fertility.

"The men naturally destined to populate the District of Maine, the vacant lands of New Hampshire and Vermont, will be enticed to the new paradise of Louisiana, which, after a few more jubilees, will throw off its allegiance to a government too distant to compel obedience, and unite with a country beyond the Alleghany in the dismemberment of the nation. The sinews of New England will be drawn out to

invigorate new settlements in countries which God and
Nature have made it impossible to unite under one government for a length of time; and *our monies* will be expended
on post roads, which, for years to come, must be chiefly
traversed by wolves and catamounts. But these mischiefs,
however fatal, and accompanied as they probably will be by
a substitution of philosophical whims for national establish-
ments, are the least which will result from the supremacy of
one State over the rest."

WHERE ARE THE NEW ENGLANDERS?

There can be little doubt that Dr. Stiles's estimate of the
future growth of the New England population was correct,
and that there are now living many more than eight million
persons who descend from the twenty-two thousand who emi-
grated from England under the lead of the Puritan Fathers;
only these millions of people are not cooped up, as he
supposed they would be, within the confines of New England.
There are, I am told, and I believe, more men and women
of New England blood in San Francisco than there are in
Boston. There are undoubtedly more persons of New England origin in Ohio than in Connecticut. Nothing is more
curious or suggestive than the census tables which show
the diffusion over every State of the persons born in New
England. Yet these tables do not show the descendants in
the second and after generations. Of these eight millions of
Dr. Stiles's estimate, which was as I suppose correct, probably
not two millions live in the three States which he assigned
as the home for eight in 1860. The other millions are scattered over all parts of this land, and other regions of the
world.

THE WORLD'S ADVANCE.

The increase of population, thus proceeding by general
laws, of which Dr. Stiles understood the formula, gives no
hint of the increase of wealth, comfort, refinement; of the
change in social order and home life; of the advance in
education, in philosophy, and the arts of life, especially in
civil order and in religion, which these hundred and twenty
years have made. Nothing is more amusing than the brag-
gart boasting of our American oratory,— its congratulations
on what has been achieved. The most amusing feature often
is, that the orator is a person who has done nothing himself
towards the advancement which he proclaims. But no

prophet of our future ever succeeds in portraying, in advance, either the method or rapidity of its progress. I happened, in early life, to see, every day, the men who, in face of the derision of the solid men of their time, were forcing the railroad system upon unwilling Massachusetts. It is not fifty years since those days. Well, in their wildest dreams of the future, there was not a man of them who looked forward to the development which we see to-day. I remember that in a speech at Faneuil Hall, my father based his estimates on a daily travel of nine persons each way between Boston and Connecticut River, and with what pleasure he told us, on his return, that the audience cried out that this was not large enough. I have the manuscript journal of one of the finest young men of New England, in which he describes with rage the sight of a cotton factory in Waltham. He looked with horror on that cruel Moloch of machinery which was, as he supposed, to be the ruin of our laboring men! For such reasons, there is no more instructive reading than a volume of the pamphlets of fifty years ago. Whatever they prophesy of evil — and of course they prophesy evil — is evil which has not come. Whatever they prophesy of good does not approach the level which has been attained. There is not the man of us, nor the woman, who has foresight enough to tell what will be the discoveries of the next ten years, nor broad enough, even if he knew them, to multiply into each other the results of these discoveries, and give to us their product as it will show itself in our civilization. And there is no one, whatever his enthusiasm for human nature, who is able to prophesy what the man of the future can do, when he shall have armor, weapons, and tools wrought out by new science in new fields, and so achieving victories now wholly unknown. Yet we are as wise as our fathers. In such ignorance as ours, then, we can see why it was that they have never, at any moment, been able to forecast the future, of which we are.

Let me say this, too, in passing : that New England has gone through more than one fundamental change in her social order in this period of one hundred and twenty years. Dr. Stiles spoke to the representatives of three colonies, who were on the eve of paying their congratulations to the young prince, George III., who that year came to the throne. There were not more loyal men in the British empire,— indeed, it would be hard to find any who expressed their loyalty with that sort of fervor that belonged to the provincialism of colonists. That generation had not passed, Dr. Stiles himself was not dead, before these very men were at work framing new constitutions of government for independent States, and laying the foundation on which this nation stands to-day. Or, take it in the appliances of physical life; take it in matters of business: Dr. Stiles spoke to men whose wealth was gathered from the seas in their fisheries, or in the commerce which they maintained with the various shores of the Atlantic. A generation had not passed before these men and their sons were carrying on the trade of the new-born nation with the East Indies and with the North-west Coast; and in a few years more they were at the head of the carrying trade of the world. Various causes, among which the sullen jealousy of the Southern States of America was foremost, crippled that trade, and in the end broke it up for years. The young Hotspurs of the South and West, under the lead of Calhoun and Clay, who were joined in this policy, meant to punish poor New England by the destruction of her commerce. Poor New England took them at their word, and built up that system of manufacture which makes the New England of to-day, of which Mr. Calhoun lived to be more jealous than ever the hottest Hotspur of his young companions was of her foreign trade. From fishermen and sailors, our people became, without knowing it, the manufacturers for this nation, and you know for how much of the rest of the world. Such have been the changes in politics and in business; as for the change in education and religion, I need not speak. There is a satisfaction in saying that some men, as Stiles did in this very address, boldly prophesied the improvement in theology which is now matter of history, and claimed wisely that in the Congregational order there was always room for more light proceeding from God's holy word.

There has been no incident of these miraculous changes more curious than that in which New England, for half a century, provided the men and women for the higher education for all parts of this country. She sent out the schoolmasters and the school-mistresses of the South and the West. The Western colleges were founded by her sons, and their first professors were educated in her schools. It is not fifty years ago that Mr. Calhoun said, in conversation, that he had seen the time, when, in the House of Representatives in Congress, the natives of Connecticut and the graduates of Yale College in Connecticut made nearly one-half of the

House, lacking only five of an actual majority. Yet at no time, I suppose, has the population of Connecticut been more than one-thirtieth part of the United States. It is twenty years ago that a French traveller, sent here on a mission by the French Government, called my attention to the system by which, as he said, Massachusetts and Connecticut educated the United States. "I have been through Canada," said he, " and through your Western States. In every State, I have found that the teachers of the schools were from Massachusetts or Connecticut. The thing is without parallel in history. There has never been a land of which it could be said that the teachers were all from the same province. I have inquired," said he, "for the statistics, that I might include them in my report to government. I have found that no one could give them to me. I have said 'When I come as far as Massachusetts, I shall find them proud of this. I can obtain these statistics there.' And now I have come here," he said, "no one knows anything about it." I encouraged him by telling him that without giving the full statistics I could obtain some details which would illustrate what he wanted. And when I next saw our dear friend, Dr. Joseph Allen, the minister of Northboro', I asked him how many of their young people who had gone West in forty years had become teachers. He seemed surprised that I should ask such a simple question, and his answer was, " Practically all of them." The simple truth is, that, in one capacity or another, every man or woman who goes into the North-west from New England devotes himself to the maintenance of a high standard of public education. And you know the consequence. The school systems of the North-west are quite as good as yours, and so is their administration. As for school-houses, they had the advantage of the liberality, more than princely, of the general government, which gave to them one-sixteenth of the proceeds of the land sales. And so, in those States which had the wisdom to use this fund for their school-houses, you may see, in towns which are only five years from prairie, school-houses as good as you have in Boston,— much better than the average district school-house of New England.

As I see Western men and men from the Pacific, though I find they may be willing to make fun of Yankee peculiarities, I never find them ashamed of Yankee blood, or unwilling to claim relationship when they can. New England is proving her likeness to Old England, as she sends out her colonies over the world. As the England of the "tight little island" sends her books, her inventions, her tools, her drumbeat, and her sons and daughters to Canada, to Australia, to New Zealand, to the Cape, and to India, so does this other England, this New England, send out her children. I do not see but that they are as loyal to their mother. And it is truly in their lives that she lives.

HOW NEW ENGLAND SHALL RETAIN HER ASCENDANCY.

But if she wishes to maintain this ascendancy, it must be by the same means which won it. She must send out her people, not one by one to take their chances of being absorbed and overpowered by their new neighbors, but in companies of men and women able and willing to bear each others' burdens. I say companies of men and women. It is the earliest distinction of New England, and one of the greatest, that the Pilgrim Fathers invented this system of colonizing. . They builded better than they knew in this, as in so many other things. The foundations of Manhattan were laid by men alone, eager to go home as soon as their engagement closed. So at Jamestown in Virginia, the first settlers were all men. Farther back yet, the unsuccessful colony of Popham was a colony of men. It would be fair to call the modern system in which the men who rule a colony go as a part of it, and go with their women and children, all determined to remain, "the New England system."

It is by such colonies, carrying with them, from the first, home, church, school, and every other requisite of society, that the power of any State extends itself. It was thus that Greece multiplied herself in the larger Greece, and Rome in the colonies which maintained the Roman Empire. Let your New Englander go alone — nay, let him go with his wife and little ones — into Virginia, into Mississippi, into Louisiana, all of which are begging him to come. The chances are that he is back again in twelve months. His wife is homesick,— he is discouraged. They laughed at him because he spoke through his nose. They were glad of his money, but they did not like his company. And she had been an outcast in her own land. But let forty of those families go together. Let them open their district school the day after their arrival. Let them hold their meeting on their first "Sabbath" under a live-oak tree. Let them sing the songs of the Lord in the strange land, and at night let them come together to tell the old stories and to dream the old

dreams. Then they carry victory with them. Not to go
back to Cutler's settlement of Marietta, or to the early histories of the Western Reserve, our own time gives noble
illustration of such successes. It was such organization of
emigration which made Kansas the State she is. It is but
twenty-five years this summer that the first settler was
admitted there. In those early years, not many more than
two thousand persons from New England went in there,—
but they were picked men and women. They went with a
principle to sustain. And they were organized from the
beginning.

That was the power which made the infant colony to be
the rock upon which broke the wave of extending slavery.
"Thus far shalt thou come, and no farther." Fourteen
years ago, the same experiment was repeated in Florida
more quietly. The same Company which had led in the
settlement of Kansas gave the information and advice which
sent into Florida several thousand emigrants from the
North-east and the North-west. No other State of the
"Confederacy" received such an infusion of Northern blood.
And that is the reason why in the election of two years ago
Florida threw her weight into the Northern scale.

Such experiments cannot be too carefully considered.
The New Englander alone, is as helpless as any other man
alone. If he is to carry with him the talisman which has
made his home the home he loves, he must carry with him
that home in institutions and organizations. He must carry
the tabernacle and the shrine and the Holy of Holies as he
has seen it in the mount, if he would not have his children
seeking for strange gods, and false, forgetting the glories,
of Zion.

And these illustrations suggest to us what is to be the true
future of New England, if she is to have any. This little
cluster of States may soon be left out in the cold,— out-
numbered, out-voted, stripped and peeled by States which
she has beaten into submission and then replaced with honor
in the national councils. But, as there are other Englands
in New Zealand, in Australia, and in India, so there are other
New Englands in Michigan, in Iowa, in Kansas, in Oregon,
and in California; and there may be others, if you and I,
and others like us, choose, in Texas and New Mexico, in
Florida,— yes, and in South Carolina. As this dreary winter
has gone by, I have had, day after day in my office, different
groups of five or six young men each, haggard and weary

with doing nothing, who had come in one by one to ask me where they should go, and what they could do. Such sense of power still attaches to the Christian Church, that men still look to its ministers to work miracles where all other means have failed. Every such day, I have said to myself what I could not say to them, Where is the Miltiades, where is the John Winthrop, where is the Manasseh Cutler, where is the Charles Robinson, to unite you together, and with you to found a new State? Where is the young gentleman of honor, of courage, and of energy enough to do what those men knew how to do, and marshal together these who are powerless to go alone? We do a great thing when we plant a college in the West, like Antioch or Oberlin. We give the West priceless treasure when we send to them our best blood, our children, one by one or two by two. But we build up our own future, we secure that supremacy of New England in this nation which this nation must enjoy if it is to live, when we send our sons and daughters,— not alone but in companies.

Such a State as Texas is to have more physical weight in this empire of ours than all these six States of New England. It is for us and our children to see that this physical force is swayed by moral power; and this is only one illustration. You heard here the message which Utah sends you, and that lovely valley of New Mexico, just now swayed by Jesuits. Another day, the message is from the Indian Territory. And each new day has its different tale. It is as she answers such appeals, or as she falls back lazily to sleep under her old-time laurels, that New England is to win her victories of the future, or to be left in history an old-time name and a respected memory.

CPSIA information can be obtained
at www.ICGtesting.com
Printed in the USA
BVHW031253270822
645678BV00011B/267

9 781167 208423